Carol Ann Tomlinson

Susan Demirsky Allan

Leadership
for
Differentiating
Schools &
Classrooms

Association for Supervision and Curriculum Development Alexandria, Virginia USA

Association for Supervision and Curriculum Development
1703 N. Beauregard St. • Alexandria, VA 22311-1714 USA
Telephone: 1-800-933-2723 or 703-578-9600 • Fax: 703-575-5400
Web site: http://www.ascd.org • E-mail: member@ascd.org

Michelle Terry, *Deputy Executive Director, Program Development*
Nancy Modrak, *Director of Publishing*
John O'Neil, *Director of Acquisitions*
Julie Houtz, *Managing Editor of Books*
Carolyn R. Pool, *Associate Editor*
Bob Land, *Copy Editor and Indexer*
Ernesto Yermoli, *Project Assistant*
Gary Bloom, *Director, Design and Production Services*
Karen Monaco, *Senior Graphic Designer*
Kimberly Lau, *Designer*
Tracey A. Smith, *Production Manager*
Dina Murray Seamon, *Production Coordinator*
Vivian Coss, *Production Coordinator*
Valerie Sprague, *Desktop Publisher*

Printed in the United States of America.

December 2000 member book (p). ASCD Premium, Comprehensive, and Regular members periodically receive ASCD books as part of their membership benefits. No. FY01-03.

ASCD Product No. 100216
ASCD member price: $19.95   nonmember price: $23.95

Library of Congress Cataloging-in-Publication Data
ISBN: 0-87120-502-5
Tomlinson, Carol A.
   Leadership for differentiating schools and classrooms / Carol Ann Tomlinson, Susan Demirsky Allan.
      p. cm.
Includes bibliographical references (p.) and index.
   ISBN 0-87120-502-5
   1. Individualized instruction. 2. Educational leadership. 3.
Classroom management. 4. School environment. I. Allan, Susan D. II.
Title.
   LB1031 .T66 2000
   371.39'4—dc21   00-011252

06 05 04 03   10 9 8 7 6 5 4 3

Leadership for *Differentiating* Schools & Classrooms

Acknowledgments · v

1 Understanding Differentiated Instruction:
Building a Foundation for Leadership · · · · · · · · · · · · · · 1

2 Reasons for Optimism About Differentiation:
Its Basis in Theory and Research · · · · · · · · · · · · · 16

3 Lessons from the Literature of Change:
What Leaders for Differentiation Need to Know · · · · · · · · 33

4 Establishing Conditions
to Initiate Systemic Change · · · · · · · · · · · · · · · · · 49

5 Practical Strategies for Implementing
a Differentiation Growth Plan · · · · · · · · · · · · · · · · 65

6 Staff Development That
Supports Differentiation · · · · · · · · · · · · · · · · · · 77

7 Continuation of Systemic Growth
Toward Differentiation · · · · · · · · · · · · · · · · · · · 87

8 Communicating with Parents and the
Public About Differentiation · · · · · · · · · · · · · · · · 103

9 Growth Toward Differentiation in Context:
A Case Study of Change in Process · · · · · · · · · · · · · 116

10 Planning for the "What" and
the "How" of Differentiation · · · · · · · · · · · · · · · · 132

Appendix · 139

References · 152

Index · 157

About the Authors · 167

▼

*With gratitude beyond any words I know to
Benzena Johnson—who is really PeeWee—angel and pit bull,
sister beneath the skin, giver of peace.*

CAT

*My work is dedicated to my spectacular family,
David, Jenny, and Brian Allan, for their love, support, and
bolstering of flagging will. My work is also for my parents, Florence
Demirsky Wolf and the late Harold Demirsky, for their love and
confidence in me. Finally, it is for the highly professional teachers
and administrators with whom I have had the privilege to work in
my career, especially those of the Grosse Pointe (Mich.) Public
Schools for their dedication to individual children and their
willingness to be among the Trailblazers.*

SDA

▲

Acknowledgments

▼

E ach day, young lives populate our schools. These young people may excel or struggle in school. They speak English or another language. They are from majority cultures, or they represent minority populations. They are male or female. They bring with them joy and optimism or trepidation and skepticism—perhaps rooted in personality or quality of home, school, and community life. Students learn eagerly or send us loud messages that our adult enterprise is not for them. They give us the better part of their waking lives for a decade and a half of their youth. What a challenge and what a trust for us as educators and leaders!

The time is right, it seems, for educators across the United States—and indeed around the world—to acknowledge that unless we deal as consciously with the differences students bring to us as we have with their similarities, we will lose too much. We will lose joy and even peace in the classroom. We will lose countless individuals. We will lose the promise of the future. And so we are eager to do it right—to figure out how to personalize our teaching—to learn to "differentiate instruction."

That enthusiasm to embrace the idea of differentiated or academically responsive classrooms is gratifying because it seems so clearly right. The feeling is frightening because it opens one more opportunity to embrace a word, be part of a movement, claim an approach that is as difficult to realize as it is powerful.

We have no recipe for reaching each young life that comes our way. Answering the inevitable and persistent challenges involved in making differentiation happen calls for risk-takers, inventors, artists, and professionals who refuse to be constrained with paint-by-number approaches to teaching. We have no recipe for changing schools. Once again, that task is for the bold among us who invent what they need but do not see. And so, if the truth be told, making changes necessary to move ourselves from pervasive one-size-fits-all teaching to something more likely to invigorate a generation of academically diverse learners is a mystery within a mystery.

We know better than to suggest that this book provides a script for success. We do hope, nonetheless, that it provides added reason to persevere, to raise questions that help thoughtful leaders be more effective and efficient in their pioneering, and to share the insights of trailblazers who have already made coherent attempts to create more academically responsive schools and classrooms.

To that end, we would like to thank a few of the restless educators, innovative thinkers, and pioneers who have charted the way in creating academically responsive classrooms. Many others whose names we don't know belong in this list as well.

Thanks to Carolyn Callahan, Tonya Moon, the continually excellent graduate students at the University of Virginia, and eager attendees whose energies have joined to make the University of Virginia's Summer Institute on Academic Diversity a learning place for all of us.

In the field, we have learned from many people in many places who are trying to make sense of both school change and differentiation. Among those who have shown us a path—worn by persistence if not clear cut by efficient machinery—are Tami Hogan and her colleagues in Sheridan, Colo.; Sandra Page, Neil Pederson, Ann Hart, Terry Greenlund, and their colleagues in Chapel Hill, N.C.; Rebecca Hayes and the highly able subject-area specialists in Fauquier County, Va.; Peg Davis in Madison, Va.; Kay Brimijoin in Amherst, Va.; education faculty and preservice teachers at Sweetbriar and Randolph Macon Colleges, also in Virginia; Chris Rauscher in Palatine, Ill.; John Artis and his coworkers in Upper Arlington, Ohio; Suette King and her colleagues in Ann Arbor, Mich.; and Jo Henderson and her colleagues in Boise, Idaho.

Over the years, we have been guided by the guidance and good counsel of Anne Lefkowitz of the Evanston (Ill.) schools, Marlene Lewis of the Dearborn (Mich.) schools, Norma Jean Sass of the Farmington (Mich.) schools, Sandra Trosien of Washtenaw (Mich.) Intermediate School District, Sylvia Whitmer of the Birmingham (Mich.) schools and the other colleagues in the "like district" group, and former colleagues of the Falls

Church (Va.) schools, particularly Mary Ellen Shaw, Janet Kremer, and Nancy Sprague (now of Fairfax County, Va.).

We have learned greatly from Bev Catlin and her colleagues in the Charlottesville City (Va.) Schools and from Mary Landrum, who quietly and intelligently set out to do the kind of work we write about here. They had no special road map—just solid preparation for the job, integrity of intent, and care in planning. Their successes were not only an illustration for us and our readers, but an encouragement as well.

A number of people in the Grosse Pointe (Mich.) school district directly contributed the products of their efforts in differentiation. Our thanks to Mary MacDonald Barrett and Christine Kaiser for their communications to parents and teachers and to Kathy Roberts for making sure that communications are written in English rather than "Educationese." We are also grateful to Jean Rusing, David King, and all the members of the elementary report card committee for their innovative work. Many other items in the book, while not directly written by members of the Grosse Pointe district, have benefited from their editing and ideas. Our thanks to Mary MacDonald Barrett, Lynn Bigelman, Paul Booker, Nicole Cole, Glenn Croydon, Marie DeLuca, Cynthia Doherty, Sonja Franchett, Barbara Gruenwald, Arlene Hicks, Mary Hooper, Jeannie Johnson, Christine Kaiser, Fran Lamb, Pamela Lemerand, Roger McQueen, Jane Nutter, Carol Peterson, Peggy Ptasznik, Grace Smith, Susan Speirs, Margaret Steele, Helen Utchenik, Martha Weaver, and many of the special education staff. Also in Grosse Pointe, we are grateful to Suzanne Klein for her unwavering support and courageous leadership; Ed Shine and all the members over the past decade of the Grosse Pointe Board of Education for having the courage to support the trailblazers; Lee Warras, mentor and friend; Roger McCaig; Alfreida Frost; the "advanced learner" group of the Grosse Pointe staff (particularly the alumni of the UVA Institute on Academic Diversity); and the building administrators and new teachers in the Orientations and New Teachers Academy, who have taught at least as much as they have learned.

Thanks also to Susan Mintz for humor and wisdom, and the example of what it means to start young teachers down a path that quests for change and responsive teaching; to Holly Gould for work with the thankless task of tracking down sources; and to Doris Standridge for enduring friendship, for creating many of the book's figures, and for bringing years of forward-looking school leadership to her editing of the manuscript.

Finally, that a book on this topic has been produced results from the belief system and incubator-like nurturing of ASCD staff—particularly those in the Program Development Work Group, with whom we have worked closely.

Understanding Differentiated Instruction: Building a Foundation for Leadership

1

L ook inside almost any classroom today and you'll see a mirror of our country. You'll find students from multiple cultures, some of whom are trying to bridge the languages and behaviors of two worlds. Students with very advanced learning skills sit next to students who struggle mightily with one or more school subjects. Children with vast reservoirs of background experience share space with peers whose world is circumscribed by the few blocks of their neighborhood. All these students have the right to expect enthusiastic teachers who are ready to meet the students as they are, and to move them along the pathway of learning as far and as fast as possible.

The reality, however, is that many of these students will encounter a teacher who is enmeshed in a system geared up to treat all 1st graders as though they were essentially the same, or all Algebra I students as though they were alike. Classrooms and schools are rarely organized to respond well to variations in student readiness, interest, or learning profile (Archambault et al., 1993; Bateman, 1993; International Institute for Advocacy for School Children, 1993; McIntosh, Vaughn, Schumm, Haager, & Lee, 1993; Tomlinson, 1995; Tomlinson, Moon, & Callahan, 1998; Westberg, Archambault, Dobyns, & a and b; Salvin, 1993). Most educators appear even to lack images of how a classroom might look—how we would "do school"—if our intent was to respond to individual learner needs. In fact, the challenge of addressing academic diversity in today's complex classrooms is as important and difficult a challenge as we have before us.

We've learned a great deal recently about how applying "differentiated instruction" can help address the needs of academically diverse learners in our increasingly diverse classrooms (see Chapter 2 for a discussion of the theory and research that supports differentiation as a way of thinking about teaching and learning). Many teachers have begun to use, or expanded their use of, the principles and practices of differentiation. To make these practices more widespread—to move from differentiation in individual classrooms to differentiation that is pervasive throughout schools and school districts—requires strong and skilled leadership.

As logical as such personalized classrooms seem, making them a reality challenges many comfortable assumptions and practices related to teaching and learning. For instance, planning for more personalized classrooms prompts an array of questions: Do our current practices make learners more independent or more dependent? What is the purpose of "standard" report cards, and are they effective? Does learning happen *in* someone or *to* them? How can we be "fair" and still respond to learner variance? How do standards and standardization differ?

We might be tempted to just cast aside, or try to forget, these sorts of professional goblins; changing practices in response to prickly insights can be troublesome. Until we face these questions, though, most students inside the classroom door will be ill served. Without large numbers of classrooms where teachers are skilled in meeting varied learners where they are and moving them ahead briskly and with understanding, the number of frustrated and disenfranchised learners in our schools can only multiply.

The purpose of this chapter is not to present an exhaustive discussion of differentiated instruction. (See the list at the end of the chapter for resources on this topic.) Rather, the chapter first reviews key vocabulary and principles of effective differentiation. The chapter then addresses some fundamental questions about differentiation that are important for people who want to establish a greater number of responsive or differentiated classrooms in their districts or schools.

Key Vocabulary and Principles of Effective Differentiation

Teachers can create differentiated, personalized, or responsive classrooms in a number of ways. Figure 1.1 presents a concept map for thinking about and planning for effectively differentiated classrooms.

Figure 1.1
A Concept Map for Differentiating Instruction

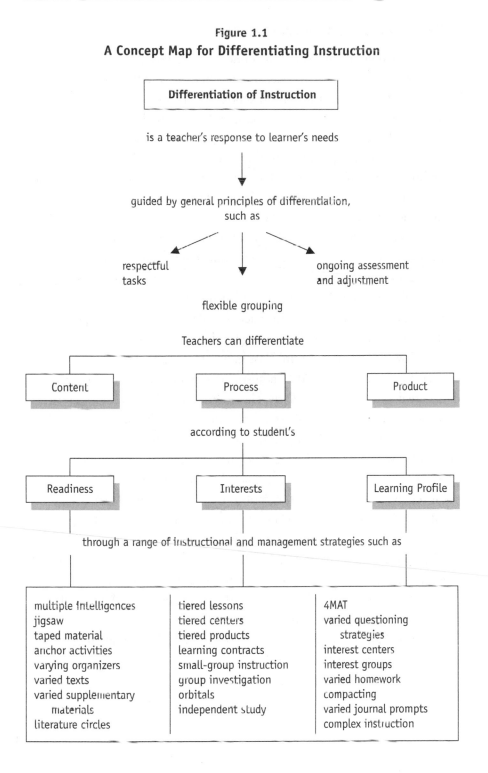

Differentiation of Instruction

is a teacher's response to learner's needs

guided by general principles of differentiation,
such as

respectful
tasks

ongoing assessment
and adjustment

flexible grouping

Teachers can differentiate

| Content | Process | Product |

according to student's

| Readiness | Interests | Learning Profile |

through a range of instructional and management strategies such as

multiple intelligences	tiered lessons	4MAT
jigsaw	tiered centers	varied questioning
taped material	tiered products	strategies
anchor activities	learning contracts	interest centers
varying organizers	small-group instruction	interest groups
varied texts	group investigation	varied homework
varied supplementary	orbitals	compacting
materials	independent study	varied journal prompts
literature circles		complex instruction

some tasks call for a grouping of students with varied learning patterns (for example, a student who learns best analytically with one who learns best through practical application). Sometimes working arrangements are simply random; students work with whoever is sitting beside them, or they count off into groups, or they draw a partner's name. Finally, in a flexibly grouped classroom, students themselves sometimes decide on their work groups and arrangements, and sometimes teachers make the call. Figure 1.2 shows the possible grouping combinations that can be achieved by mixing all the options between "levels" of the three-tiered diagram. Flexible grouping used consistently and purposefully has a variety of benefits: opportunity for carefully targeted teaching and learning, access to all materials and individuals in the classroom, a chance for students to see themselves in a variety of contexts, and rich assessment data for the teacher who "auditions" each learner in a wide range of contexts.

Figure 1.2
Flexible Grouping Options

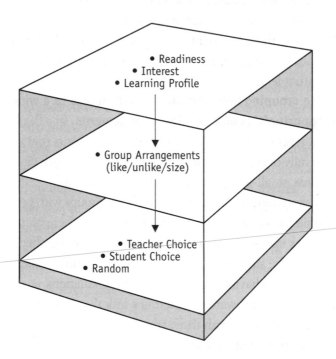

• **All students consistently work with "respectful" activities and learning arrangements.** This important principle provides that every learner must have tasks that are equally interesting and equally engaging, and which provide equal access to essential understanding and skills. In differentiated classrooms, a teacher's goal is that each child feels challenged most of the time; each child finds his or her work appealing most of the time; and each child grapples squarely with the information, principles, and skills which give that learner power to understand, apply, and move on to the next learning stage, most of the time, in the discipline being studied. Differentiation does not presume different tasks for each learner, but rather just enough flexibility in task complexity, working arrangements, and modes of learning expression that varied students find learning a good fit much of the time.

• **Students and teachers are collaborators in learning.** While the teacher is clearly a professional who diagnoses and prescribes for learning needs, facilitates learning, and crafts effective curriculum, students in differentiated classrooms are critical partners in classroom success. Students hold pivotal information about what works and does not work for them at any given moment of the teaching-learning cycle, they know their likes and preferred ways of learning, they can contribute greatly to plans for a smoothly functioning classroom, and they can learn to make choices that enhance both their learning and their status as a learner. In differentiated classrooms, teachers study their students and continually involve them in decision-making about the classroom. As a result, students become more independent as learners.

Elements of Curriculum That Can Be Differentiated

Content. A teacher can differentiate content. Content consists of facts, concepts, generalizations or principles, attitudes, and skills related to the subject, as well as materials that represent those elements. Content includes both what the teacher plans for students to learn and how the student gains access to the desired knowledge, understanding, and skills. In many instances in a differentiated classroom, essential facts, material to be understood, and skills remain constant for all learners. (Exceptions might be, for example, varying spelling lists when some students in a class spell at a 2nd grade level while others test out at an 8th grade level, or having some students practice multiplying by two a little longer, while some others are ready to multiply by seven.) What is most likely to change in a differentiated classroom is how students gain access to core learning. Some of the ways a teacher might differentiate access to content include

• Using math manipulatives with some, but not all, learners to help students understand a new idea.

• Using texts or novels at more than one reading level.

• Presenting information through both whole-to-part and part-to-whole approaches.

• Using a variety of reading-buddy arrangements to support and challenge students working with text materials.

• Reteaching students who need another demonstration, or exempting students who already demonstrate mastery from reading a chapter or from sitting through a reteaching session.

• Using texts, computer programs, tape recorders, and videos as a way of conveying key concepts to varied learners.

Process. A teacher can differentiate process. Process is how the learner comes to make sense of, understand, and "own" the key facts, concepts, generalizations, and skills of the subject. A familiar synonym for process is *activity.* An effective activity or task generally involves students in using an essential skill to come to understand an essential idea, and is clearly focused on a learning goal. A teacher can differentiate an activity or process by, for example, providing varied options at differing levels of difficulty or based on differing student interests. He can offer different amounts of teacher and student support for a task. A teacher can give students choices about how they express what they learn during a research exercise—providing options, for example, of creating a political cartoon, writing a letter to the editor, or making a diagram as a way of expressing what they understand about relations between the British and colonists at the onset of the American Revolution.

Products. A teacher can also differentiate products. We use the term *products* to refer to the items a student can use to demonstrate what he or she has come to know, understand, and be able to do as the result of an extended period of study. A product can be, for example, a portfolio of student work; an exhibition of solutions to real-world problems that draw on knowledge, understanding, and skill achieved over the course of a semester; an end-of-unit project; or a complex and challenging paper-and-pencil test. A good product causes students to rethink what they have learned, apply what they can do, extend their understanding and skill, and become involved in both critical and creative thinking. Among the ways to differentiate products are to:

- Allow students to help design products around essential learning goals.
- Encourage students to express what they have learned in varied ways.
- Allow for varied working arrangements (for example, working alone or as part of a team to complete the product).
- Provide or encourage use of varied types of resources in preparing products.
- Provide product assignments at varying degrees of difficulty to match student readiness.
- Use a wide variety of kinds of assessments.
- Work with students to develop rubrics of quality that allow for demonstration of both whole-class and individual goals.

Student Characteristics for Which Teachers Can Differentiate

Students vary in *at least* three ways that make modifying instruction a wise strategy for teachers: Students differ (1) in their readiness to work with a particular idea or skill at a given time, (2) in pursuits or topics that they find interesting, and (3) in learning profiles that may be shaped by gender, culture, learning style, or intelligence preference.

Readiness. To differentiate in response to student readiness, a teacher constructs tasks or provides learning choices at different levels of difficulty. Some ways in which teachers can adjust for readiness include

- Adjusting the degree of difficulty of a task to provide an appropriate level of challenge.
- Adding or removing teacher or peer coaching, use of manipulatives, or presence or absence of models for a task. Teacher and peer coaching are known as *scaffolding* because they provide a framework or a structure that supports student thought and work.

• Making the task more or less familiar based on the proficiency of the learner's experiences or skills for the task.
• Varying direct instruction by small-group need.

Interest. To differentiate in response to student interest, a teacher aligns key skills and material for understanding from a curriculum segment with topics or pursuits that intrigue students. For example, a student can learn much about a culture or time period by carefully analyzing its music. A social studies teacher may encourage one student to begin exploring the history, beliefs, and customs of medieval Europe by examining the music of the time. A study of science in the Middle Ages might engage another student more.

Some ways in which teachers can differentiate in response to student interest include

• Using adults or peers with prior knowledge to serve as mentors in an area of shared interest.
• Providing a variety of avenues for student exploration of a topic or expression of learning.
• Providing broad access to a wide range of materials and technologies.
• Giving students a choice of tasks and products, including student-designed options.
• Encouraging investigation or application of key concepts and principles in student interest areas.

Learning Profile. To differentiate in response to student learning profile, a teacher addresses learning styles, student talent, or intelligence profiles. Some ways in which teachers can differentiate in response to student learning profile include

• Creating a learning environment with flexible spaces and learning options.
• Presenting information through auditory, visual, and kinesthetic modes.
• Encouraging students to explore information and ideas through auditory, visual, and kinesthetic modes.
• Allowing students to work alone or with peers.
• Ensuring a choice of competitive, cooperative, and independent learning experiences.

- Balancing varied perspectives on an issue or topic.
- Providing authentic learning opportunities in various intelligence or talent areas.

As you can see, differentiation of content, process, and products is achievable in each of the areas of student readiness, interest, and learning profile.

Instructional Strategies That Facilitate Differentiation

Instructional strategies are tools of the teacher's art. Like all tools, they can be used artfully or clumsily, appropriately or inappropriately. The person who uses them determines their worth. No instructional strategy can compensate for a teacher who lacks proficiency in his content area, is unclear about learning goals, plans an unfocused activity, or does not possess the leadership and management skills to orchestrate effective classroom functioning.

Nonetheless, a teacher who is comfortable and skilled with the use of multiple instructional strategies is more likely to reach out effectively to varied students than is the teacher who uses a single approach to teaching and learning. Teachers are particularly limited when the sole or primary instructional strategy is teacher-centered (such as lecture), or drill-and-practice (such as worksheets).

Numerous instructional strategies invite attention to student readiness, interest, and learning profile. Among these strategies are learning centers, interest groups, group investigation, complex instruction, compacting, learning contracts, tiered activities, tiered products, rubrics constructed jointly by teacher and student, use of alternative forms of assessment, and many others. (For more information on instructional strategies that support differentiation, see Tomlinson, 1999, *The Differentiated Classroom: Responding to the Needs of All Learners*, listed in the resource section at the end of this chapter.)

By sharing a common vocabulary and beginning with a common set of principles related to differentiation, school leaders have more tools to provide guidance and direction for all staff members as they begin the journey toward developing more academically responsive classrooms.

Additional Reflections about Differentiated Classrooms

Attending to learner variance and need historically has made common sense in a classroom. This approach also reflects decades of proliferating knowledge about the brain, learning styles and varieties of intelligence, the influence of gender and culture on how we learn, human motivation, and how individuals construct meaning. Teachers and school leaders who spend time in a classroom *see* the significant array of learner differences. People who study the scholarship of this field *understand* differences and the need to attend to them, if we are to serve properly the children and families who trust us.

All evidence aside, however, moving away from the sense that we ought to personalize our classrooms to *doing* something substantial about it is devilishly difficult. Setting out to develop a significant number of responsive, personalized, or differentiated classrooms in our schools is an educational change of monumental proportions. Therefore, the purpose of this book is to explore how school leaders can encourage and support such significant changes in our classrooms.

Beyond the general framework and principles of differentiated instruction are at least three additional considerations for educators who desire to provide leadership in differentiation. These interrelated considerations provide a compass for our journey.

First, differentiation that is rooted in ineffective classroom practice cannot succeed. Trivial and fluffy curriculum remains trivial and fluffy even after differentiation. Varied versions of an ill-focused product are no more helpful. A pernicious classroom environment cannot invite learners to be comfortable with themselves and one another. A teacher who does not see assessment as a continual window into the needs of her students has little sound footing from which to differentiate instruction. A teacher who cannot learn to trust and share responsibility with her students would, at best, have students seated in rows and completing *varied* worksheets silently and alone. Perhaps the most singular truth about providing leadership for differentiated classrooms is that you should often feel as though you are moving backwards rather than forwards! You need to spend time reflecting on and providing leadership in the fundamentals of effective teaching when or before you provide leadership in the more sophisticated skills of differentiation.

Second, differentiation is more than a strategy or series of strategies—it is a way of thinking about teaching and learning. In other words, facilitating teacher growth in differentiation is not so much about introducing tiered lessons, independent study, alternative forms of assessment—or even moving to multitext adoption. Practicing quality differentiation is much more about knowing what matters to teach, realizing that learning happens in us rather than to us, continually reflecting on the "particularness" of each of our students, and pondering how to develop both the commonalities students share as humans and the singularities students bring as individuals. If we as teachers understood the nature of our art more fully and deeply, more differentiation would likely evolve from that understanding. Learning some new "tricks" with little sense of why they matter is less helpful.

Third, movement toward differentiation in teaching is movement toward expertise. Regarding differentiation, teachers can say, "I already do that." Most teachers at some times and in some ways obviously adapt or adjust for students' learning needs. The truly expert teacher understands, however, that even after a dozen careers in the classroom, he could still learn more about his subject and his learners and how to link each learner and subject with power and joy. In truth, providing effective leadership for differentiation fosters the sort of continual growth teachers need throughout their classroom lives in order to help each learner build the best life possible. Effective leadership for differentiation comes from dogged, unremitting insistence on and support for the fact that expert teachers teach students the most important things in the most effective ways. The mission of effective leadership is to maximize the number of expert teachers in a school's or district's classrooms.

One goal of this book is to provide very practical guidance in how to be an effective leader in establishing more differentiated classrooms and more effectively differentiated classrooms. Remember, however, that practicality is necessarily rooted in understanding and vision.

A Look Ahead

With this vocabulary and these beliefs in mind, we have developed this book to help educational leaders think through the complexities of guiding substantial change in classrooms at the school and district levels. In Chapter 2, the book examines potential positive outcomes of differentiation based on theory, research, and less formal observation. Chapter 3 provides an overview of what literature on school change reveals about practices that impede and facilitate change in schools and districts. Chapter 4 looks at key conditions at the initiation of school or district movement toward differentiation. Chapter 5 examines practical strategies useful in the implementation stages of growth toward differentiation, while Chapter 6 spotlights the imperative of effective staff development programs to undergird differentiation efforts. Chapter 7 discusses key considerations in the continuation stage of change, as differentiation becomes more common in a school or district. Chapter 8 takes a look at communicating with parents and the public about differentiation. Chapter 9 details a case study of a district involved in a serious and focused change effort for differentiated classrooms, allowing a look—in context—at many of the principles and practices discussed elsewhere in the book. The last chapter in the book presents a final challenge for educational leaders as they provide guidance and support for developing a growing number of classrooms capable of addressing the academic diversity that typifies today's schools and will typify schools in the years ahead. We hope you enjoy thinking along with us!

To Learn More About the Principles and Practices of Differentiation

Note: See also References at the end of this book, as well as additional resources in several chapters.

Bearne, E. (Ed.). (1996). *Differentiation and diversity in the primary school.* New York: Routledge.

Buswell, B., Schaffner, C., & Seyler, A. (1999). *Opening doors: Connecting students to curriculum, classmates, and learning.* Colorado Springs: PEAK Parent Center, Inc.

Kiernan, L. (Producer). (1997). *Differentiating instruction* [A video staff development set]. Alexandria, VA: Association for Supervision and Curriculum Development.

Madea, B. (1994). *The multiage classroom: An inside look at one community of learners.* Cypress, CA: Creative Teaching Press.

Tomlinson, C. (1995). *How to differentiate instruction in mixed ability classrooms.* Alexandria, VA: Association for Supervision and Curriculum Development.

Tomlinson, C. (1996). *Differentiating instruction for mixed-ability classrooms* [A professional inquiry kit]. Alexandria, VA: Association for Supervision and Curriculum Development.

Tomlinson, C. (1999). *The differentiated classroom. Responding to the needs of all learners.* Alexandria, VA: Association for Supervision and Curriculum Development.

Winebrenner, S. (1992). *Teaching gifted kids in the regular classroom.* Minneapolis, MN: Free Spirit Publishing.

Winebrenner, S. (1996). *Teaching kids with learning difficulties in the regular classroom.* Minneapolis, MN: Free Spirit Publishing.

Reasons for Optimism About Differentiation: Its Basis in Theory and Research

2

ise educators and educational leaders ask questions about options that affect their professional practice. *Why might we adopt one path over another? Where do the ideas in a particular approach come from? What reason do we have to believe an approach would make classrooms and schools better and more productive places?* In addition, a skeptical public increasingly asks school leaders to cite evidence that instructional approaches are sound. This chapter addresses some of the questions and evidence related to the approach we refer to as "differentiation of instruction."

To look at the "root system" of differentiated instruction, we study three areas of interest. First, we look at some of the beliefs that undergird the approach of differentiation. Then, we examine some of the educational theory that supports differentiation. Finally, the research stemming from differentiation provides at least an early sense of the possibilities of differentiated or responsive instruction.

Differentiation Is a Response to Beliefs

What we label as differentiated instruction is not a new phenomenon. The first teacher who stood amidst a group of students amazed and intrigued by the variation among them was perhaps the first practitioner of differentiation in the classroom. Perhaps the concept of differentiation dates back even further: to parents who first understood that what works in guiding one child does not always work when guiding a sibling.

Further, differentiation is not really one entity, but rather synthesizes a number of educational theories and practices. Bringing those theories and practices together helps teachers address their classroom activity in a manner that is more holistic than fragmented.

Behind differentiated instruction, however, lies a set of beliefs about teaching and learning. Among those beliefs are the following:

- Human beings share common feelings and needs, and schools should help us understand and respect those commonalities.
- Individuals also differ significantly as learners; these differences matter in the classroom, and schools should help us understand and respect the differences.
- Intelligence is dynamic rather than static, plural rather than singular.
- Human capacity is malleable, and the art of teaching is the art of maximizing human capacity; a central goal of schools ought to be maximizing the capacity of each learner.
- We probably underestimate the capacity of every child as a learner.
- Students should be at the center of the learning process, actively involved in making sense of the world around them through the lenses we call "the disciplines."
- All learners require respectful, powerful, and engaging schoolwork to develop their individual capacities so that they become fulfilled and productive members of society.
- A major emphasis in learner development is competition against oneself for growth and progress.
- Teachers and other adults need to help learners accept responsibility for their own growth and progress.
- Individuals and society benefit when schools and classrooms are genuine communities of respect and learning.
- Effective heterogeneous classrooms are essential to building community in our schools.
- Effective heterogeneous classrooms are powerful venues because most students spend most of their school time in such classrooms.
- All effective heterogeneous classrooms recognize the similarities and differences in learners and robustly attend to them.
- Excellent differentiated classrooms are excellent first and differentiated second.

While each of these statements is grounded in our ongoing understanding of education, each statement is more one of philosophy or belief than an outgrowth of test-tube data. Leaders need to reflect on the meaning and implications of these beliefs and to extend the list's scope and possibilities. Each district, school, and classroom also should examine the degree to which it reflects or rejects each of the beliefs. Clearly our educational system grants us the privilege of disagreement. The belief system of one person need not replicate someone else's. On the other hand, differentiated instruction can probably not take root or thrive in a setting where the beliefs just listed are deemed inappropriate.

Differentiation Is Rooted in Educational Theories

The model of differentiated instruction advocated here rests upon an active, student-centered, meaning-making approach to teaching and learning. Such approaches are often called "constructivist." Many people have written about this approach to education, including John Dewey, Jean Piaget, and Jerome Bruner, and more recently, Brooks and Brooks (1993), Erickson (1998), and Wiggins and McTighe (1998). For purposes of brevity, this section does not examine constructivist theories, although certainly we would encourage educational leaders to explore these in depth using the wealth of available sources. Instead, in this book we look at theories supporting differentiation by readiness, interest, and learning profile: the three key elements of differentiation itself.

Background for Readiness Differentiation

Psychology and contemporary brain research both offer the theory that individuals learn in accordance with their "readiness" to do so. That is, "Tasks must be at the proper level of difficulty to be and to remain motivating: tasks that are too easy become boring; tasks that are too difficult cause frustration" (National Research Council, 1999).

The Russian psychologist Lev Vygotsky (1962, 1978) describes a sort of personal arena in which learning takes place. At a certain point of skill and understanding related to a given facet of learning, explains Vygotsky, a child can function totally independently. Beyond that point, a task is too difficult for a child to proceed alone. However, when a teacher scaffolds or supports the child in moving through somewhat more complex applications, the child can succeed. Further down the continuum of task complexity, children become frustrated and unable to function successfully even with adult support. The area in which a child cannot successfully function alone but can succeed with adult scaffolding or support is that child's "zone of proximal development." In that range new learning takes place—when the task is just a little too hard for the child, but when adult support provides guidance for success. The teacher's job is to push the child into his or her zone of proximal development, coach for success with a task more complex than the child can manage alone, and thus push forward the area of independence. Through repetition of such cycles we grasp new ideas, master new skills, and become increasingly independent thinkers and problem solvers. Because of both developmental and experiential differences, not all children of the same age have the same zones of proximal development in regard to a particular understanding or skill.

Brain research appears to affirm what psychologists such as Vygotsky propose. Revealing the physiology behind the psychology, brain researchers (Howard, 1994; Jensen, E., 1998) explain that learning occurs when the learner experiences neither boredom nor anxiety—when he or she is neither overchallenged nor underchallenged. Describing a state much like Vygotsky's zone of proximal development, brain researchers speak of "moderate challenge" and "relaxed alertness." Both terms echo the need for challenge and support for the learner.

> The consensus of a broad range of psychologists and brain researchers is that: Instruction should always "be in advance" of a child's current level of mastery. That is, teachers should teach within a child's zone of proximal development. If material is presented at or below the mastery level, there will be no growth. If presented well above the zone, children will be confused and frustrated (Byrnes, 1996, p. 33).

Background for Interest Differentiation

Psychologists suggest that interest is a doorway to learning. The topics we are interested in become a priority for us, and we attend to them. Linked to motivation, student interest can be a compelling factor in learning, because interest makes tasks engaging, satisfying, and personally challenging. When interest is tapped, learning is more likely to be rewarding, and the student becomes a more autonomous learner (Bruner, 1961).

Further, creativity is highest when skills of a given domain combine with a student's own interests and creative thinking processes. Students who are encouraged to pursue areas of interest are likely to tap into—and increase—skills important to a particular subject discipline. Clearly interest-based options seize on intrinsic motivation. In addition, by giving students some latitude in how they pursue interest-based learning, teachers empower students to exercise creative thinking. By helping students discover and pursue their passions, we can maximize their engagement with learning, their productivity, and their individual talents (Amabile, 1983; Collins & Amabile, 1999).

Csikszentmihalyi and Csikszentmihalyi (e.g., 1988) pose a theory of flow: a state of total absorption that comes from being lost in an activity that is so satisfying that the participant loses track of time, weariness, and everything else but the activity itself. A key requirement for flow is the interest of the participant in the activity. Being involved in flow is so pleasing that people who experience it generally are willing to do whatever it takes to produce the feeling again, including sustained hard work.

Interestingly for the concept of differentiation, Csikszentmihalyi (1990) notes that other conditions for flow are clarity about the purpose or goals of the task (a key element of effective instruction), and the participant's sense that the task is within his or her capacity to act (match between learner skills and the task, or readiness). The search for flow leads to escalating complexity as the participant seeks new challenges and opportunities to apply growing skills and understanding in the context of the interesting pursuit. An interest that prompts flow also fosters the skills necessary for development of one's talents: curiosity, concentration, emotional independence, and persistence.

Background for Learning Profile Differentiation

The model of differentiation we have described envisions "learning profile" as including learning style, intelligence preference, and influences of gender and culture. Together, these elements speak not to the speed or depth with which we learn nor to what we are interested in learning, but rather to how we learn as individuals. Over time, numerous psychologists and educators have proposed theories related to each of these components.

Dunn (e.g., 1996) is among educators who have proposed that individuals vary in preference for conditions of learning. Dunn suggests four learning-style categories: environmental, emotional, sociological, and physical. Her work proposes that individual preference for such factors as quiet or background noise, bright light or low light, formal or informal seating, sustained concentration or shorter periods of concentration, perceptual mode (auditory, visual, kinesthetic), time of day for learning to occur, degree of responsibility, relationships to peers, and degree of mobility can influence student achievement and attitude about learning.

Many other theorists have written about the connection between learning style and learner success. (A helpful digest of such work is available in Sternberg & Grigorenko, 1997.) Although their lenses for thinking about learning style differ, theorists generally agree that while learning preferences vary over time and with different conditions, some degree of learning-style preference is likely biological. Even individuals in the same family vary in learning style. Matching learning-style preference and conditions of learning is considered one way to improve learning.

Best known among theorists regarding intelligence preference are Howard Gardner (e.g., 1983) and Robert Sternberg (e.g., 1985). Both psychologists offer theories of "multiple intelligences," or the idea that human intelligence manifests itself in many spheres of human endeavor. Gardner proposes eight potential intelligences: verbal-linguistic, logical-mathematical, visual-spatial, bodily-kinesthetic, musical-rhythmic, interpersonal, intrapersonal, and naturalist. Sternberg proposes three: analytical, creative, and practical. While the two theories differ in some key ways, both theorists believe that intelligence is a capacity to solve problems or produce products valued by the society in which an individual lives. Gardner and Sternberg also propose that human intelligence is fluid rather than fixed, and that functional human beings operate in more than one intelligence sphere, while having strengths or preferences in one or more. In addition, both theorists suggest that teaching should attend to an individual's intelligence preferences.

Finally, numerous sociologists, psychologists, and educators have written about learning differences that appear to stem from gender and culture. Understanding the effect of gender and culture on learning requires more space than is available here. Embedded in a person's gender and culture are subtle ways of functioning that can profoundly affect how a person sees and interacts with the world, including the classroom. A mismatch occurs when a person who is socialized to act one way through his or her gender or culture finds that the classroom is predicated on a different set of assumptions and attitudes.

In general, for example, some theorists maintain that females appear to (1) prefer collaborative rather than competitive learning opportunities, (2) communicate for purposes of establishing relationships, and (3) have a preference for areas of study that appear to facilitate helping others. By contrast, males may prefer competition (including communication for competition rather than for establishing relationships), and more analytic subjects such as science and math (see Gilligan, 1982; Tannen, 1990). Such propositions always come with the caveat that generalizing about all members of a given gender is dangerous. Many males, for example, prefer collaborative learning, and many women communicate for power or competition.

Culture shapes the intangible aspects of a person's life: perspectives, points of view, frames of reference, modes of communication (nonverbal as well as verbal), and sense of identity. In regard to culture, theorists propose, for example, that one's cognitive style is influenced by culture. Members of Western cultures may be more competitive, oriented to individual achievement, rigid about time, restricted in affective expression, task oriented, and have a preference for part-to-whole thinking, whereas members of non-Western cultures may be more oriented to group achievement, flexible about time, open about affective expression, socially oriented, and have a preference for whole-to-part thinking (see Lasley & Matczynski, 1997).

Again comes the caution that recognition of cultural patterns can easily become stereotyping, and clearly not all members of any cultural group are alike in a given way. Furthermore, most people are members of many different cultures or microcultures and thus are shaped in multiple ways (Banks, 1994).

Scholars propose that the instructional materials, curriculum, staff attitudes and beliefs, policies, teaching styles, assessment procedures, and other facets of schools may be advantageous to members of some gender or cultural groups and disadvantageous to others (Banks, 1993; Delpit, 1995). Some social classes likely benefit or do not benefit as well. The result is that teachers and administrators misinterpret a student's behavior or misalign learning opportunities because they don't understand the student's learning and communication styles as shaped by her cultural tradition (Garcia, 1998).

Research Support for Differentiated Instruction

Once again, because the model of differentiated instruction advocated in this and related publications is an amalgamation of beliefs, theories, and practices, research supporting the model also comes from a variety of sources. An exhaustive look at related research is beyond the scope of this chapter. Providing some illustrative samples of a much broader set of research, however, can be useful. Again, the model's emphasis on differentiation by readiness, interest, and learning profile provides the format for presentation of research findings.

Sample Research Related to Readiness Differentiation

Many sources point clearly to the need for learning tasks to match student readiness. Only a few are mentioned here.

A continuous line of research conducted by David Hunt and his associates since the 1960s has established that more effective learning takes place when the amount of task structure provided by a teacher matches a student's level of development (e.g., Hunt, 1971). A related study shows a relationship between student achievement and a teacher's ability to diagnose the student's skills level and prescribe appropriate tasks (Fisher et al., 1980).

In a study of 250 classrooms, researchers found that in classrooms where individual students worked at a high success rate, they felt better about themselves and the subject they were studying, as well as learning more (Fisher et al., 1980). Echoing the idea of the zone of proximal development, studies suggest that a success rate of about 80 percent (or a bit higher if students have to work quite independently) seems optimum for growth (Berliner, 1984, 1988; McGreal, 1985). The researchers focus squarely on the principle of differentiation for student readiness with their caution that student achievement is not likely to improve when teachers ask students to practice that which they already know (to function at too high a success rate), and that student achievement is likely to be negatively affected when teachers ask students to complete tasks that cause students ongoing frustration (to function at too low a success rate).

A strong body of research addresses multigrade classrooms, which by intent and necessity are differentiated. One research review of quantitative studies found students in multigrade classrooms outperforming students in single-grade classrooms on 75 percent of measures used (Miller, 1990). These findings may be particularly revealing because the focus of multiage classrooms is typically not student performance on test results, and achievement tests used were typically designed for single-grade settings (Bingham, 1995). Another review of research literature noted that multigrade students were superior to single-grade counterparts in study habits, social interaction, cooperation, and attitude toward school, while performing as well or better on achievement tests (Gayfer, 1991). In a study of nongraded classrooms (which bear many similarities to multiage settings) standardized tests were used to compare academic achievement in 57 of 64 settings reviewed. In these studies, 58 percent favored students in nongraded settings, 33 percent found nongraded settings to be as effective as graded settings, and only 9 percent favored graded settings. Mental health components of the studies reviewed favored nongraded settings as well. Further, 17 longitudinal studies favored nongraded settings, with the suggestion that effects become more positive the longer students stay in such settings (Anderson & Pavan, 1993). Studies have demonstrated the effectiveness of the multiage model in serving as a catalyst for teachers to rethink the nature of teaching and learning (Maehr & Midgley, 1996).

In a fascinating and complex five-year longitudinal study of 200 teenagers (Csikszentmihalyi, Rathunde, & Whalen, 1993), researchers pursued the question of why some teenagers become committed to the development of their talents while others become disengaged from developing their talents. Included among the study's many findings is the necessity of a match between the complexity of tasks developed by teachers for students and the individual skill level of a student. Students whose skills were underchallenged demonstrated low involvement in learning activities and lessening of concentration. Conversely, students whose skills were inadequate for the level of challenge demonstrated both low achievement and a plummeting of self-worth. Most destructive was the combination of low-challenge tasks and a low student sense of exercising skills. "This situation, which accounted for almost a third (29 percent) of classroom activities, consisted mostly of reading, watching films, and listening to lectures" (p. 186). According to these researchers, essentials for attention, motivation, and development of one's capacities in school are opportunities for meaningful action and the skills necessary to act successfully. Teachers effective in developing student talent crafted challenges commensurate with student readiness levels.

These studies and similar research not reviewed here support the differentiation principle of adjusting tasks to learner readiness. In differentiated classrooms, teachers ensure that a task is appropriately challenging for the readiness of a given learner by modifying the degree of learner dependence or independence, the degree of task clarity or "fuzziness," the degree of structure or openness of a learning task, or by teaching or reteaching particular skills in small groups as students need them. Research suggests that such teacher adjustments can enhance both student achievement and student attitudes about learning.

Sample Research Related to Interest Differentiation

The work of numerous researchers reveals the importance of fostering individual interest as a means of enhancing motivation, achievement, and productivity (e.g., Amabile, 1983; Torrance, 1995).

> The freedom to choose what to work on allows individuals to seek out questions that they are highly intrinsically motivated to pursue. This high level of intrinsic interest will lay the groundwork for creative achievement. Teachers may incorporate this approach into the classroom by allowing students to choose their own topics for individual or group projects (Collins & Amabile, 1999, pp. 305–306).

Such motivation can be maintained over time if teachers and parents systematically engage students in discussing the pleasure of creativity and the joy of learning, and if adults maintain environments where learners feel free to exchange ideas and share interests (Hennessey & Zbikowski, 1993).

Not surprisingly, student interest also takes center stage in the research findings of Csikszentmihalyi and colleagues (1993) noted in the previous section. Student interest in a task was as key to talent development as was the match between task complexity and student readiness for the task. Not only do the researchers explain that student interest is key to ongoing student motivation to pursue tasks of ever-increasing complexity, but also that student interest in and satisfaction stemming from earlier tasks is often key to continued student engagement in work that is momentarily not interesting. Students who were uncommitted to developing their talents did not find work in their talent area interesting or involving, and the students did not see a connection between their talent areas and their futures. By contrast, students committed to developing their talents were far more likely to find tasks in their talent areas to be interesting, and also far more likely to see a connection between their current work and future goals. The researchers conclude that these findings call upon teachers to establish instructional conditions that develop full student interest and involvement in learning. The researchers say that these conditions include establishing classroom environments where students are known, their particular interests are recognized and valued, and teachers provide work suited to those interests. Results from this study—related to both readiness/skills match and the role of interest in learning—contribute to an understanding of flow discussed briefly in the theory section of this chapter (Csikszentmihalyi, 1990). This study found that flow (peak moments of absorption in work) was the strongest predictor of student engagement and of how far a student progressed in the school's curriculum and in talent development.

Many other researchers have similarly found that when students are interested in what they study, an important positive influence on learning exists in both the short term and the long term (e.g., Hebert, 1993; Renninger, 1990). One educator/researcher conducted empirical research on the role of student interest in learning and concludes:

> The best learning environment is like a good cafeteria. It not only affords the essential staples but also offers a large variety of choices to satisfy individual tastes. This allows children to discover their natural interests, proclivities, and special talents (Jensen, A., 1998).

Sample Research Related to Learning Profile Differentiation

Learning profile refers to ways in which a student best processes information and ideas, and ways in which learning style, gender, culture, and intelligence preference influence the student. Research in each of these four categories suggests that being sensitive to learning profile provides benefits for instruction.

Numerous researchers over a period of decades have concluded that addressing an individual's learning styles through flexible and compatible teaching results in increased academic achievement. In a meta-analysis of research on the effect of learning-style accommodation, Sullivan (1993) found that accommodating learning style through complementary teaching or counseling interventions resulted in significant academic and attitude gains for students from all cultural groups.

The powerful educational and anthropological research of Lisa Delpit (1995) makes a convincing case for how classrooms in which students' cultural differences are misunderstood or ignored can have a negative effect on students. Delpit suggests that the following factors can seriously undermine the academic success of students from many minority groups:

- Subtle differences in communication style.
- Conferring and responding to status.
- Role of feelings and need for emotional closeness in learning.
- Need for affiliation vs. achievement.
- Need for contextualized vs. decontextualized learning.
- Need for doing vs. talking.
- Need for movement in a classroom.

As one small example, she points to a culturally influenced communication difference that must make classrooms seem bizarre to students of non-Caucasian backgrounds. A prevalent communication pattern in many classrooms is for teachers to ask young students to name an object, tell its color, or report the number of objects present. Students from African American backgrounds may well be puzzled by this teacher behavior because in their homes, adults typically ask children for information only when the adult does not have the information. Similarly, she found Japanese American students conflicted by an assignment to spell out their line of logic in a speech (tell them what you're going to say, say it, and tell them what you said). In the culture of many of these students, such a speech would be insulting. A speaker does not repeat what an audience already knows. To do so is offensive. The assignment, clear and appropriate for some students in the class, compromised other students who had to choose between honoring their teacher and honoring their culture.

Conversely, other studies have reported a positive effect on addressing students' learning profiles on elementary students, secondary students, students with learning disabilities, and students with emotional handicaps, among other groups. Additional learning-styles research has found positive effects of instruction matched to learning styles on numerous cultural groups, including Native American, Hispanic, African American, Asian American, and Caucasian students. (For a useful summary of this research, see Dunn & Griggs, 1995, pp. 37–78.)

Virtually all research on learning style includes the caution that considerable diversity of learning style exists in every cultural group and in both genders. The goal of addressing learning style in differentiated classrooms is not to assign tasks to students based on culture or gender, but rather to establish instructional environments in which students, whatever their gender or culture, find a match to preferred modes of learning on a consistent basis. "The question is not necessarily how to create the perfect 'culturally matched' learning situation for each ethnic group, but rather how to recognize when there is a problem for a particular child and how to seek its cause in the most broadly conceived fashion" (Delpit, 1995, p. 167).

Of keen importance in supporting attention to student intelligence preference in classroom instruction is the research of Robert Sternberg (e.g., Sternberg, 1997; Sternberg, Torff, & Grigorenko, 1998). Studies continue to find that when students are matched to instruction suited to their learning patterns (e.g., analytic, creative, practical), they achieve significantly better than comparable students whose instruction is not matched to their learning patterns. This conclusion holds true for primary grade, middle school and high school students. In fact, states Sternberg, "Even by partially matching instruction to (learning patterns), we could improve student achievement" (1997, p. 23).

Sternberg and his colleagues conclude (Grigorenko & Sternberg, 1997) that learning profile adds to our understanding of students' performance and should be taken into account in classrooms in both instruction and assessment. "[T]he diversity of styles among students implies that students need a variety of means of assessment to maximize and show to an optimal extent their talents and achievements" (p. 310). Nonetheless, for example, 3rd and 8th graders taught with a learning profile match learned more than students taught with either a traditional memory-based approach or with analytically based instruction. Further, the learning gains resulted in both memory-based assessments already in place in the districts studied, as well as on performance-based assessments created for the study (Sternberg et al., 1998). In other words, students taught with this particular multiple-intelligence approach performed better, even on conventional measures, than students taught conventionally.

Positive effects of teaching with a multiple-intelligence focus based on the work of Howard Gardner (e.g., 1983) are also documented, although generally less rigorously than the Sternberg research. For example, Campbell and Campbell (1999) write about increased test scores for students in six schools with very different demographics (two elementary, two middle, and two high schools) as a result of a multiple-intelligence focus in instruction. Of particular note is that students from varied cultural and economic groups all seemed to flourish academically in these settings. Both students and staff in these schools reportedly found a new enthusiasm for teaching and learning as a result of the multiple-intelligence focus as well. Both achievement and attitude gains are linked to a belief that undergirds differentiated instruction: No single approach works with all students. Classrooms work best when students and teachers collaborate to develop multiple avenues to learning.

In a study based on the work of Gardner, researchers also found for teachers and parents benefits of a multiple-intelligence focus (Tomlinson, Callahan, & Lelli, 1997). Teachers in a large district who developed classrooms with a multiple-intelligence approach demonstrated more flexibility in teaching and more student-centered instruction than did peers not involved in the study. Further, participating teachers were able to see and act upon possibilities in nontraditional learners (e.g., those initially weaker in verbal and mathematical readiness) in ways that teachers found difficult prior to the study. Finally, participating teachers were more able to communicate positive messages to parents about their children, which in turn made the parents more receptive to school and participation in school-related events.

Looking at Differentiation as a Whole Model

To this point, the chapter has provided a sampling of theory and research related to the parts of the model advocated in this and related publications. The question remains: How effective are classrooms that bring together what we know (or think we know) about addressing readiness, interest, and learning profile into a coherent and proactively planned whole?

At this point, the answer is that studies are new and evidence is just beginning to be examined. Anecdotal reports of the full model of differentiation are very promising. Test scores rose markedly in a middle school in Anchorage, Alaska, that took a schoolwide approach to differentiation. A charter school in Canada that practiced the model reported similar results. A high school science teacher who conducted action research on the effect of differentiation on achievement of his students found positive gains. Numerous teachers have written about improved achievement, as well as engagement and attitude gains in their own differentiated classrooms. These reports, while encouraging, are not the carefully designed studies that are necessary to understand both positive and negative features of applying the whole model of differentiated instruction. (Research studies such as those cited earlier in the chapter in multiage classrooms *do* carefully examine results of broadly applied approaches to addressing individual learning needs in classrooms.)

One research survey at the middle grade level documented conditions that speak to the need for more responsive classrooms (Tomlinson, Moon, & Callahan, 1998). Two research studies have examined the effect of implementing the full differentiation model, particularly as the model relates to teacher change (Callahan, Tomlinson, & Moon, in press-a; Tomlinson, 1995). These three studies are particularly pertinent for leaders attempting to understand the complexity and effect of this sort of change initiative on teachers and schools.

Back to the Beginning

If the question is whether we have research evidence to support the effort to create more academically responsive classrooms, the answer is: yes, we do. Do we need more research? Of course, and part of what is needed is careful examination by individual teachers and schools of the effects—both positive and negative—of implementing differentiation. We need to look always at academic outcomes for varying students in varying settings. Academic outcomes include standardized test-score gains, but such outcomes should also include the following results:

- Evidence of quality of work.
- Mental and affective engagement.
- Interest in school.
- Degree of student self-efficacy.
- Growth of each student in comparison with self.
- Evidence of complex thinking and problem solving.
- Any other indicators that give us insight into how well we are crafting and delivering curriculum and instruction that cause each student to develop his or her capacity consistently and vigorously.

We ought also to look at indicators of success such as school attendance, developing sense of community inside the classroom and beyond, discipline referrals, parent involvement in and satisfaction with school, and other factors that let us know how well we are doing in creating student-friendly classrooms and schools.

In the end, classrooms are complex and messy places. Research that tells the full story about any classroom, school, district, or approach to teaching is also predictably messy, complex, difficult to come by, and nearly always equivocal. Such is the nature of the teaching-learning enterprise.

Thus, in the final analysis, we will necessarily return to the assertion that we differentiate instruction because we cannot do otherwise. We know too much about student variance to pretend that it does not exist or that it is unimportant. We know too much about the art of teaching to assume it can happen effectively in template fashion.

A staff developer recently wrote a letter reflecting the frustration of some high school teachers faced with the suggestion that they somehow personalize their instruction, when 150-plus students revolve through their classrooms every day. Asked the staff developer, "What do I say to them?" There is really only one answer: "You try." A Native Alaskan educator said it simply, "In order to teach you, I must know you" (Delpit, 1995).

Pat Carini (in Ayres, 1993) reminds us there is no way to know any individual student fully, but that educators should stay "open to mystery, to the recognition that there is always more to know and more to allow students their full humanity, and to stay alive as a teacher" (p. 49).

Educators who believe Carini's assertion will continue working to enact it in their schools and classrooms, and continue the quest not just for evidence that responsive teaching works, but for evidence of what makes it work best.

Lessons from the Literature of Change: What Leaders for Differentiation Need to Know

3

All of the suggestions and illustrations in this book stem from two sources. First, they have been effective in particular schools and districts. Second, they are rooted in a growing understanding of what promotes positive change in schools. That a particular strategy has worked in the world of education is reassuring. Alone, however, such success is not enough to guarantee, or even to suggest, that the same approach will bring about widespread or positive change in other places. Indeed, copying success is not easy to do in the educational arena.

While our instincts, common sense, and the experiences of others may compel us as leaders to attempt to bring about changes in classrooms, the chances that our good intentions will bear good fruit are slim at best unless we are informed about how change works (or doesn't work) in schools. The purpose of this chapter is to provide some key insights about what is important in leading for significant school change, and to relate those insights to the topic of differentiated instruction. At the end of the chapter is a list of excellent books on educational change. Each of the books is fascinating and important reading for educational leaders who want to make a difference in their profession. While we hope to clarify some essential principles of school change, this chapter cannot substitute for a deeper, ongoing study of this very important field.

To summarize change theory, we've selected nine fundamental points about change in schools and we relate them here to leadership for differentiation. All of the principles are implicit or explicit in other parts of the book. The relationship of these principles to effective leadership for differentiated classrooms is so vital, however, that we want to bring them together in one place for direct comment. In each instance, we'll spotlight the principle, synthesize insights about the principle, and briefly comment on its implications for educators who want to be catalysts for developing more responsive, student-friendly, or differentiated classrooms that are rooted in our best understanding of teaching and learning. The nine principles are as follows:

- Change is imperative in today's classrooms.
- The focus of school change must be classroom practice.
- For schools to become what they ought to be, we need systemic change.
- Change is difficult, slow, and uncertain.
- Systemic change requires both leadership and administration.
- To change schools, we must change the culture of schools.
- What leaders do speaks with greater force than what they say.
- Change efforts need to link with a wider world.
- Leaders for change have a results-based orientation.

Principle 1: Change Is Imperative in Today's Classrooms

In general, we know change is necessary for growth. Whatever does not change does not grow, and what does not grow atrophies. This correlation holds true for individuals, for systems, and for educators and the schools where they spend their professional lives. Change is a precondition for continued existence.

Further pointing the way to change is the compelling knowledge we have developed in recent generations about how students learn. We have a clear sense of what would characterize high-quality practice in a classroom. Many of our classrooms, however, look remarkably like those of 100 years ago: places where teachers tell, students repeat, and facts alone seem to map the universe of knowledge. Thus, we need to change, to apply our best understanding of teaching and learning to classrooms. Just as we demand that medicine, architecture, engineering, and even sports must be contemporary, classrooms, too, must be contemporary.

We also have learned much about students' learning styles, intelligence varieties, and the effects of gender and culture on learning. We understand the role of choice in motivation and the role of motivation in achievement.

We know that individuals must learn from their own starting points or readiness levels rather than from a generic point of understanding. We know that diversity of all sorts—academic, cultural, and economic—is proliferating in schools and classrooms. We also have a well-defined sense of what is needed in classrooms to prepare students for life in a new century that will, in many ways, be markedly different from the century in which their parents and grandparents attended school. Many students spend great portions of their lives in today's schools feeling marginalized by classrooms that seem to cast them as inferior if they struggle with school, already smart enough if they come to school ahead, problematic if they speak a language other than English, and perverse if they question the school agenda. "A different way to learn is what the kids are calling for. . . . All of them are talking about how our one-size-fits-all delivery system—which mandates that everyone learn the same thing at the same time, no matter what their individual needs— has failed them" (Sarason, 1990, pp. 114–115). We need to change in order to craft schools where we earn each student's trust that his or her particular capacities will be maximized.

In addition, teachers feel as frustrated and alienated in stagnant schools as do the students who attend them. We cannot afford to lose large numbers of experienced educators to discouragement, exhaustion, and guilt. Nor can we afford to retain teachers who continue in their classrooms lost in discouragement and anger. Revitalized schools would revitalize teachers and students as well.

Why change? Because we become irrelevant if we do not. It's as simple (and complex) as that. Where does differentiation fit into the mandate for change? We cannot have high-quality schools that effectively develop productive and engaged learners in the absence of responsive classrooms. It's as simple (and complex) as that.

Principle 2: The Focus of School Change Must Be Classroom Practice

The sort of change we need to revitalize students, teachers, and schools necessarily has one focus—creating classrooms where each student is coached in becoming the best educated, most productive person possible. Philip Schlechty (1997) reminds us that

The business of schools is to design, create, and invent high-quality, intellectually demanding work for students: schoolwork that calls on students to think, to reason, and to use their minds well and that calls on them to engage ideas, facts, and understandings whose perpetuation is essential to the survival of the common culture and relevant to the particular culture, group, and milieu from which students come and in which they are likely to function (pp. 50–51).

Schlechty reminds us, too, that artful teaching involves attracting students to learning—making learning irresistible, even when the task at hand is not inherently interesting to the learner. Figure 3.1 suggests characteristics of schoolwork that ought to be central to all school change efforts.

Many classrooms stand in contrast to the characteristics listed in Figure 3.1. Specifically,

• Most of us as teachers (including former teachers who are now administrators) are ill-prepared to structure and deliver high-quality classrooms. Teachers must develop the knowledge, tools, skills, and practices necessary to structure and deliver these sorts of environments.

• Teachers' worlds provide little time for reflection, observation, or discussion of their current state of the art, or to envision more promising ways of practicing their profession.

• Left to their own devices, most teachers would not be likely to find or take the opportunity to become reflective problem solvers and change agents in their own classrooms.

Efforts at school change that do not call upon teachers, and engage in partnerships with them, to develop the sorts of high-quality schoolwork that Schlechty describes are unlikely to span the gap between what schools are and what they ought to be. We thus ought not adopt block scheduling, for example, as a focus of change per se. The question that marches before change and creates its cadence is, "How might we ensure that we are developing important, mentally and affectively engaging schoolwork for each child in this district, school, and classroom?" If block scheduling can help do that (and indications are that it can), then we may elect to use block scheduling—not because of its popularity, but because we are clear on how it would join with other facets of best-practice instruction to make learning more compelling for more students and their teachers.

Figure 3.1
Characteristics of High-Quality Curriculum and Instruction

High-Quality Curriculum and Instruction

• Is clearly focused on the essential understandings and skills of the discipline that a professional would value.
• Is mentally and affectively engaging to learners.
• Is joyful—or at least satisfying.
• Provides choices.
• Is clear in expectations.
• Allows meaningful collaboration.
• Is focused on products (something students make or do) that matter to students.
• Connects with students' lives and world.
• Is fresh and surprising.
• Seems real (*is* real) to the student.
• Is coherent (organized, unified, sensible) to the student.
• Is rich, deals with profound ideas.
• Stretches the students.
• Calls on students to use what they learn in interesting and important ways.
• Involves the students in setting goals for their learning and assessing progress toward those goals.

Similarly, moving toward differentiated classrooms makes sense only as we see how differentiating or personalizing instruction maximizes the capacities of more and more learners. The innovation or change is not the goal, but rather a means to a broader end.

Teachers are highly unlikely to develop exemplary instruction in the absence of responsiveness to student readiness, interest, and learning profile. Take notice, however, that differentiating low-level, nonengaging classroom activities is relatively futile.

The implication of Principle 2 for differentiation is twofold. First, no other curricular reform can fulfill its potential without recognizing, embracing, and proactively addressing variance in student readiness, interest, and learning profile. Thus differentiation (by whatever name, or no name at all) must be a focus of school change. Second, efforts we might tout as differentiation that are not persistently rooted in the broader context of a relentless pursuit of dynamic curriculum and instruction are likely not worth the effort of teachers or administrators.

Principle 3: For Schools to Become What They Ought to Be, We Need Systemic Change

Undeniably a teacher here or a team there can achieve expertise in designing and facilitating effective differentiation. Most parents of children in such a classroom would be grateful for the benefits offered in those singular environments. A student in one of those classrooms could experience life-transforming change. In no way would we want to discourage the evolution of individual teachers in becoming skilled at designing and leading responsive or differentiated classrooms.

On the other hand, pockets of quality do not seem to spread on their own. A mission of educational leaders is widespread dissemination of excellent practice: promoting broad-scale quality. To fulfill that mission, leaders need to understand

- Changing a few individual classrooms won't add up to school change.
- Changing individual schools won't add up to district change.
- Shared knowledge and experiences of educators across classrooms and schools are essential to shared growth and purpose among educators.
- Promoting widespread (systemic) change requires a district-level vision, constancy of direction, and action over a sustained period of time.
- Centralized mandates for change are only one step in promoting change. By themselves, mandates are too little to affect enduring change, but they are not unimportant. Mandates rooted in a vision, action, and support are often essential catalysts for change.
- Centralized vision, direction, and action do not strip power from individual schools and classrooms. Rather they serve as compasses for change—providing a destination while encouraging schools and individuals to be creative in determining the best means for reaching the destination.

An implication for differentiation of principle No. 3 is that if responsive teaching is to become widespread enough to make a difference in the school experiences of today's heterogeneous school populations, districtwide efforts are required. Widespread and effective differentiation does not happen by accident. The act of encouraging and supporting *individual* teachers in learning to differentiate instruction is useful for a few teachers, but that plan is inadequate for creating academically responsive schools or districts.

Principle 4: Change Is Difficult, Slow, and Uncertain

Change is unnerving. The prospect of change makes us feel uncomfortable, often guilty. It challenges us, makes us rethink ourselves, calls on us to recreate what we do. Change robs us of certainty, routine, and all the comforts to which we would rather cling. Consequently, people resist change, even when we see the need for it—let alone when we are unconvinced of a need. Change agents should reflect on the following comments on change, many of which apply specifically to education:

• Many teachers and administrators are skeptical of the need for change in schools and even more skeptical that it will happen.

• Leaders contribute to skepticism about change when they adopt and then abandon new initiatives in rapid-fire succession. In districts with bandwagon histories, teachers know that if they wait a bit, the call for a particular change eventually passes.

• Change creates tension and conflict. An absence of problems in a school or district may well suggest that little growth is required.

• People commonly adopt as little change as possible.

• Teachers often believe they have changed when they have not.

• No one right answer exists for change. Because schools and districts harbor multiple perspectives and belief systems, change creates tension among educators.

• Gaining the understanding and skills required for change takes time. Teachers have no time.

• Knowledge and skills required for change must be developed within teachers. Teachers must own knowledge and skills, not simply receive them or borrow them from superordinates. Coming to "own" new ways of thinking and acting is a slow process.

• Unlearning old ways of thinking and doing is often as difficult as learning new ways of thinking and doing.

• In the midst of change, situations often become a lot worse before they become a lot better.

If teachers are to learn to develop more academically responsive classrooms, leaders must understand that leadership for the change has no end date. Not only do current administrators and teachers require career-long upgrading of their beliefs and practices in order to reach a high level of sophistication with differentiation, but new administrations and teachers are continually coming on board who have to start at the beginning of understanding the principles and practices of differentiation. In the meantime, tension exists as teachers are asked to abandon comfortable, if ineffective, ways of viewing learners, learning, and teaching. Awkwardness and failures persist as teachers grapple with new perceptions and practices. Leaders may prefer to give up rather than to proceed; but when leaders give up, they contribute to the nearly universal teacher belief that change is a synonym for "fad," that innovations have the shelf life of bread, and that business as usual is fine after all.

Principle 5: Systemic Change Requires Both Leadership and Administration

In instances where positive changes have taken root and flourished in school districts (and in schools), dream keepers and managers—both leaders and administrators—have generally been essential to the change. The same individual may play the two roles in part or in whole, but the two roles are quite different. Each is essential.

Leadership for innovation requires a person with a vision and the capacity to extend it to others. A leader for change

• Articulates a vision based on moral and professional purpose.
• Inspires others to think along with her.
• Listens to the ideas of others and incorporates them into the vision as appropriate.
• Gains acceptance for the vision.
• Teaches followers.
• Helps others work through the difficult passages of change.
• Focuses on maintaining a sense of direction over an extended period of time.

• Is an active participant in the change process, accepting responsibility for outcomes rather than merely assigning responsibility to others.

Administration for change plays a management role. The manager or administrator role includes

• Making plans to ensure that abstract visions for change become concrete.
• Taking care of budgets, schedules, access to materials and knowledge, and organization of other resources necessary for change.
• Working with teachers and administrators to determine their needs related to the change process, and responding effectively and efficiently.
• Formally assessing both the process of change and its outcomes.

When systemic change is a goal, both dream keepers and stewards of the dream are a necessity. Another key player in systemic change is a school level leader; generally that person is the principal. If the principal is not a viable person for this role, the principal should designate someone to fill the bill as school leader. Everyone in the change process must recognize that the designee speaks with the full blessing and backing of the principal. The principal (or other school-level leader) typically performs the following functions:

• Makes the vision a daily reality in the context of the school and classroom.
• Coaches for change.
• Guides individuals and the faculty as a whole in working on smaller facets of a larger vision with the goal of tempering tension and frustration as well as ensuring steady and observable successes.
• Deals with issues of accountability at a classroom level.
• Serves as a confidant for teachers and other building administrators related to the change.
• Articulates to district leaders and managers needs, feelings, and progress of school-level educators.
• Engages in team-building for change.
• Ensures that teachers are appropriately supported in and recognized for their efforts toward change.

• Helps district leaders and managers maintain coherence between the goal of change and daily policies and procedures.

District leaders and administrators are obligated to provide adequate support (including time, understanding, materials, recognition, etc.) for those asked to lead at the school level. School-level leaders are obligated to provide (or ensure) adequate support for teachers and administrators of whom change is requested. Leaders at all levels do not just direct or permit, they empower (Schlechty, 1997).

A critical need in districts seeking significant change is stability among leaders at all levels. Even under the best of circumstances, when establishing widespread consensus for change, the effect on a change initiative is profound and negative when dream keepers, administrators, or school-level leaders change. Just as widespread change may take as long as 7 to 10 years or more, long-term commitment of change leaders to their roles is of prime importance. Positive change is most likely when key district-level administrators stay in their roles for 6 years or more (Fullan, 1999). Indications are that stability is no less important for school-level leaders.

As with all major change initiatives in schools, significant progress toward effectively differentiated classrooms calls for a visionary who can inspire others to look at individual learners, to understand their possibilities and needs, and to craft classrooms well suited to addressing multiple needs. Movement toward effective differentiation also calls for a person to ensure that day-to-day actions give feet to the dream. Teachers shouldn't be asked to change their worlds unless reliable partners provide resources, such as rich and extended staff development opportunities, time for thought and collaborative planning, extra hands to help with the early stages of classroom management in a multitask classroom, and so on. Also necessary is a school-level leader with the power to effect change, monitor progress, serve as a bridge between school and district, build links among classrooms, facilitate teaching partnerships among generalists and specialists, and so on.

As a corollary, both mandates and invitations must precede widespread change. Asking a teacher—who may be a good issuer of invitations, but who will never have any clout—to make differentiation happen beyond his own classroom is inappropriate.

Principle 6: To Change Schools, We Must Change the Culture of Schools

"If only we could provide staff development that links closely to the classroom, teaching practices would change, and schools would evolve as classrooms changed." Studies of school change suggest that this assumption is faulty.

We have deeply entrenched ways of thinking about learners and learning, deeply embedded ways of "doing school." Schools are cultures governed by norms, traditions, and mores. From concrete images of how classrooms should be arranged to more abstract issues of how we think about student success and failure, how we "do school" is as much a part of our life maps as how we celebrate a given holiday.

Further, each educator brings into the profession beliefs about children, about the roles of adults in children's lives, about fairness and justice, and about various economic and ethnic groups. These beliefs, too, are part of our culture as individuals and as educators. We may or may not be conscious of the attitudes, beliefs, and habits that permeate how we think about and practice our profession, but their influence is profound.

Neither changes in policy nor changes in school structures are likely to be adequate to change our beliefs. Informed leaders for change understand that

• Change efforts must include ongoing attempts to understand why teachers and administrators practice as they do, not merely attempts to change practice without regard to beliefs.
• Teachers may, over time, come to new beliefs through new actions.
• Opportunity is important in the change process.
• Opportunities to reflect on and discuss embedded beliefs need to occur at the faculty level and the individual level.

In regard to leadership for differentiation, many artifacts and beliefs about school will likely need to be examined to make way for sustained change. Promoting effective differentiation is difficult—mandates notwithstanding—if educators' beliefs include the following:

• Teachers are tellers and students are absorbers.
• Time in the classroom is fixed.

- Curriculum is largely fact based and skill based.
- Pleasurable learning is a luxury.
- "Fair" means treating all kids alike.
- Students don't learn what the teacher doesn't directly oversee.
- Life is difficult, and teachers must help students prepare for its rigors by giving them a taste of "reality" in the classroom.
- Sorting of students through grading and scheduling is appropriate and effective.
- If we'd just homogeneously group students, we wouldn't need differentiation.
- Intelligence is fixed.
- Ability and compliance are intertwined.
- Most students cannot handle responsibility in the classroom.
- Most students should be able to learn in the same way.
- Students who differ broadly from grade-level expectations are problematic.
- Students who achieve above grade level are already fine and we don't need to worry about them.
- Student deficits are generally at fault when students don't learn.

Such beliefs are common. Many teachers and administrators who hold them may never have articulated them, and we might even be uncomfortable doing so. Yet if such beliefs are part of the culture of the teacher or the school, the idea of academically responsive classrooms makes little sense.

A wise leader for differentiation assists educators in probing the beliefs behind their actions, developing new classroom practices, and encouraging educators to use the new practices as new lenses for looking at students, teaching, and learning. New practices and old beliefs are often incompatible, and the power of the old beliefs is such that they will win the day unless the old beliefs evolve to make sense of new practices.

Principle 7: What Leaders Do Speaks with Greater Force Than What They Say

Effective leaders understand that they are in the environment-building business. Change that occurs does so against the odds. Critical to beating the odds is establishing an environment that balances the necessity for change with an atmosphere that supports change. Further, an educational leader is a mirror of a larger culture that is reflected in the classroom. In other words, as leaders, we ought not do what we would not want teachers to do in their classrooms. In this regard, an effective change agent

- Balances mandates with winning trust and commitment.
- Respects the differences among staff members and builds on them in positive ways.
- Creates opportunities for teachers and administrators to build a sense of community.
- Works against "good guy" (complier)/"bad guy" (noncomplier) dichotomies.
- Continually nurtures the growth and professionalism of individuals.
- Promotes risk-taking by creating safe and fear-free settings.
- Designs a satisfying learning process for teachers to continually expand their capacities.
- Builds opportunities for teacher success and recognizes that success.
- Allows their own vision to grow through collaboration with others.
- Promotes development of creative solutions to problems.

An effective leader for differentiation understands that she plays the same role with teachers that teachers play with their students. Such a leader should continually model effective differentiation for and community building among teachers. In fact, leaders for differentiation should talk with teachers about the parallels between teacher learning at the school level and student learning at the classroom level, calling attention to such parallel factors as

- A common learning objective with different routes of achieving it.
- Preassessing readiness and moving ahead from readiness points.
- Varied opportunities to make sense of and express new learning.
- Drawing on teacher interest and learning profile.
- Flexible timetables for growth and change.
- Joint goal-setting and assessment of progress by leader and learner.
- Varied opportunities to learn with and from peers as well as individually.

• Acknowledging individual growth.

• Respecting individual differences in the context of a community of varied learners.

Principle 8: Change Efforts Need to Link with a Wider World

Leaders for change understand that efforts to promote change cannot stop at the schoolhouse doors. Folks beyond those doors need instruction from those of us whose professional lives are lived in school—and to teach us as well. Effective leaders accomplish the former by helping parents and community members understand and develop confidence in the vision of more productive classrooms—by helping parents and community members develop an evolving sense of the possibilities of schools. Such leaders accomplish the latter by ensuring that parents and community members help schools understand students better through "seeing" them in their communities and homes.

Involving community calls for a sense of balance in leaders. Parents and community members have agendas for schools. Sensitive leaders hear and incorporate the agenda—but often in ways that extend beyond the particulars—find and seize upon common visions and yet extend the horizons of possibility.

Leaders for differentiation must surely help parents both understand the concept of differentiation and experience benefits for their own particular children. At the same time, leaders for differentiation involve parents in sharing with classroom teachers their depth of knowledge about their own children in an atmosphere of mutual respect. Similarly, both parents and community members involve themselves in assessing the effectiveness of change and providing resources for improvement. While attending carefully to *what* parents and community members want for their children, effective leaders fashion *how* the dreams can be realized in ways that honor the hopes of all segments of the community while honoring the hopes of individuals as well.

Principle 9: Leaders for Change Have a Results-Based Orientation

Just as effective teachers continually monitor the progress of learners in a variety of ways and adapt instruction appropriately based on their assessments, effective leaders for change constantly look for both formal and informal indicators of growth and progress in the area of change. Such leaders understand

• The ultimate goal of the change is increased student engagement in learning, student understanding, and student capacity to apply what has been learned to settings inside and outside the classroom.

• Teacher change needs to precede student change.

• Both teacher growth and student growth need to be monitored.

• Different school constituencies are interested in different results.

• No single measure is robust enough to tell the whole story of teacher or student growth.

• Single measures of growth or measures that overlook key features of growth have negative effects on the change process.

Further, results-oriented leaders help teachers and faculties examine indicators of growth, reflect on the meaning of the evidence, and determine implications for both school and individual practice.

Once again, this principle has direct bearing on change for more academically responsive classrooms. An effective leader for differentiation seeks, through a variety of means, evidence of change and its implications for students and teachers. Such a leader continually revises staff development plans, use of time and other resources, and short-term goals based on evidence of growth. The leader communicates to various constituencies evidence meaningful to them. Finally, he consciously models and discusses the parallels between results-based leadership and a results-based differentiated classroom.

Neither Formulas nor Dark of Night

Change is difficult because it is riddled with dilemmas, ambivalences, and paradoxes. It combines steps that seemingly do not go together: to have a clear vision and be open-minded; to take initiative and empower others; to provide support and pressure; to start small and think big; to expect results and be patient and persistent; to have a plan and be flexible; to use top-down and bottom-up strategies; to experience uncertainty and satisfaction (Fullan, 1991, p. 350).

There is no recipe, no blueprint for change. On the other hand, embarking on change is not slogging into a swamp in the dark of night. We know a lot about change, and this knowledge is rich with humanity and common sense. A wise leader for school change—in regard to differentiation or another change initiative—is armed with available knowledge, as well as humanity and common sense. Wishing or even mandating change does not make it come to pass. Though more difficult than that, the journey *is* possible; and as is true with most things in life, the complex and uncertain things are often the most rewarding.

To Read More About Change in Schools

Fullan, M. (1991). *The new meaning of educational change* (2nd ed.). New York: Teachers College Press.

Fullan, M. (1993). *Change forces: Probing the depths of educational reform.* London: The Falmer Press.

Fullan, M. (1999). *Change forces: The sequel.* London: The Falmer Press.

Hong, L. (1996). *Surviving school reform: A year in the life of one school.* New York: Teachers College Press.

Sarason, S. (1990). *The predictable failure of educational reform.* San Francisco: Jossey-Bass.

Sarason, S. (1996). *Revisiting the culture of school and the problem of change.* New York: Teachers College Press.

Schlechty, P. (1997). *Inventing better schools: An action plan for educational reform.* San Francisco: Jossey-Bass.

Establishing Conditions to Initiate Systemic Change

4

Having established a background for thinking about differentiation, we turn our attention now to the sorts of plans that leaders must make and put into action if change is to happen broadly across schools and districts, rather than in scattered individual classrooms. This sort of broad change is called systemic change. Promoting systemic change toward differentiation is the goal of this book.

An individual classroom teacher, without any system or school support, can take steps toward differentiating instruction in his or her classroom. Many teachers have done so. Even within a single classroom, however, moving toward a philosophy of accommodating academic diversity and individual needs generally constitutes a change. The likelihood that a teacher will be able to make such a significant change—even within the confines of his own classroom—is greatly enhanced by accompanying change in the school culture as a whole. At the very least, a sense of support and approval from the administration goes far to encourage classroom change. More powerful support is provided by alterations in the organizational structure that are catalysts for classroom changes. Therefore, the task of the school leader—whether a school administrator or central office staff member—is to design systemic strategies that encourage teachers to implement differentiated instruction in the classroom and that support teachers in honing the skills of differentiation.

Systemic strategies change existing school systems and school structures in order to make differentiation for individual students and groups of students more likely. Systemic strategies can include more common accommodations, such as ensuring a full array of support personnel with expertise in special education, gifted education, reading, or language; and less common accommodations, such as making multiple grade-level resources available in a single classroom, providing "looping" or multiage options, creating flexible groupings across classrooms, modifying report cards, planning coherent staff development programs, and others we examine as the book progresses. These systemic strategies require district- or school-level modifications and contrast with classroom strategies (such as flexible grouping, independent studies, interest centers, tiered lessons, compacting, multiple intelligence approaches, and so on) that an individual teacher can implement to differentiate instruction.

A comprehensive plan for implementing differentiated instruction includes both systemic and classroom strategies. This book focuses on *systemic* strategies that ultimately encourage differentiation *within* classrooms containing learners with varying needs.

Setting the Stage for Systemic Growth in Differentiation

One helpful strategy is to look at the change process as four stages: initiation, implementation, continuation, and outcomes (Fullan, 1991). In the real world of schools, of course, change is seldom so linear. Staff turnover and the inevitable influx of new parents necessitate that as we move ahead we are retreating to square one. Further, leaders must continue to revisit and refine their early thinking and planning, even in the later stages of change. Strategies that were useful in one stage of the change process may find a different use in later phases. Nonetheless, the four-stage framework helps us organize and assess our actions. In this chapter, we discuss key components of initiating change toward more effective differentiation. Subsequent chapters examine strategies for implementation and explore topics related to continuation and outcomes.

Actions at the Initiation Stage

How do we maximize the likelihood that many teachers will become more sensitive and responsive to student differences in their classrooms? What steps would we need to take to have parents become allies in developing effectively differentiated classrooms? What are the hallmarks of effective differentiation, and how would we know if we achieved it? These questions have no easy answers. Taking time to reflect on them and plan with them in mind, however, greatly enhances the likelihood that differentiation might establish deep roots and become a part of the district's culture.

Here, we review 10 steps or actions leaders would do well to consider in the early stages of planning for systemic movement toward differentiated instruction. These actions are

- Establish a need and articulate a vision.
- Establish common definitions and terms.
- Build understanding and support among stakeholders.
- Link differentiation and best practice.
- Focus district initiatives.
- Attend to competing mandates.
- Plan for leadership and support.
- Allocate financial resources.
- Look ahead to assessing progress.
- Plan for the long haul.

1. Establish a need and articulate a vision. While educators clearly experience student differences, that experience by itself is likely not enough to cause us to embrace changes in our habits and practices. Particularly difficult is convincing teachers or schools of the need to be more attentive to varied learner needs when those teachers or schools are already perceived to be "good." Leaders continually need to seek ways to communicate that until every student is growing and successful, our own growth as educators is unfinished. Be sure to share both research-based reasons and the needs of your own students as part of your rationale for change. A part of successfully initiating change for differentiation also entails articulating in writing (as well as orally) both the direction in which the school or district should move and the rationale for doing so.

The initiation stage of change prompts several questions (Schlechty, 1997): Why is this change needed? What kind of change is needed and what does it mean for us when the change comes about? Is what we are being asked to do really possible? Has it been done before? By whom? Where can we see it in action? How do we make the change? What skills do we need and how will they be developed in our school or district?

While no tidy answers to those questions are available, failure to consider them and to plan with them in mind diminishes the power of our efforts. An honest, clear, defensible, and compelling need and vision must define who and what the school or district wants to become. A visionary who uses the bully pulpit often and effectively must also keep the need and vision before all stakeholders. Certainly more than one leader needs to "own" and speak to the vision—but a leader at the apex of influence in the school or district has a great opportunity to inspire and focus others with a carefully conceived and thoughtfully articulated vision.

2. Establish common definitions and terms. When first hearing about differentiation, many teachers respond, "We already do that." While teachers are being honest with their answers, frequently what they are doing is "tailoring" (Shulman, 1987) instruction by the occasional use of choice in projects, modifying questions based on perception of student need. Some teachers even provide modest coaching when it is evident that an assignment is not working for a particular child. What the teacher perceives as differentiation is not proactive or planned in that the teacher does not yet regularly seek to understand student differences and modify instruction based upon analysis of student need. Tailoring may also not be a systematic and regular part of planning. Making certain that everyone is aware of the same definition and descriptors of differentiation reduces misunderstanding. In addition, adopting a framework for differentiation (such as the one depicted in Figure 1.1) establishes a common vocabulary, focuses staff development, reinforces sharing among teachers, and provides a basis for evaluating efforts.

3. Build understanding and support among stakeholders. Although your efforts may not begin with grassroots support, building stakeholder support is important for success, even in the beginning. Some teachers, upon their first encounter with the concept of differentiation, feel that someone has finally given voice to what they have always believed. In their enormous relief to reduce the isolation of teaching by having located soulmates, these instructors may be among your most vociferous early supporters. Parents also are a natural support group, since they are already likely to see their children as individuals. Effective groups of supporters not only serve as a voice for differentiation, but they also play a key role in helping uncover flaws in planning or executing plans to support differentiation. Supporters are also important in evolving an increasingly sound vision for differentiated curriculum and instruction.

Honest interaction with skeptics and antagonists about needs and plans is also crucial. Hearing beyond the anger of such individuals and groups in order to understand their fears can help leaders plan for success, and can, over time, develop a sense of trust among teachers, parents, and community members that their thoughts are valued and taken into account, even when they disagree.

4. Link differentiation and best practice. Truly effective differentiation is rooted in the best that we know of teaching and learning. Such classrooms are student-centered, hands-on, high-level, and meaning making. Teachers are clear on learning goals, and those learning goals carry with them the power of knowledge, understanding, and skill that a given discipline should develop in all learners. Respect is evident for each learner, and teacher and student together develop an environment likely to help each student grow as far and as fast as possible.

These characteristics define any excellent classroom. From these underpinnings, robust and effective differentiation evolves. In fact, differentiation simply addresses an additional key facet of classroom excellence: adapting sound instruction for individual or small-group need. For that reason, meaningful attempts at differentiation always have to begin with examination of the quality of instruction on a given day, in a given unit, or over the span of a given year. Differentiation should not be presented as something "extra" that teachers do, but rather as one hallmark of teacher quality.

Administrators and teachers should see differentiation as a nonnegotiable hallmark of teacher excellence and expertise. Differentiation is not a strategy or an add-on, but rather a way of thinking about teaching and learning that reflects a high level of teacher professionalism. Differentiation is not something an educator "already does" fully, nor can it be mastered in a year or two. A district initiative that undergirds development in the skills of differentiation needs to examine the career-long development of every teacher in a school or district.

Figure 4.1 (based on the work of educators such as Brandt, 1998, and Schlechty, 1997) shows a draft of a document that leaders in one school district developed as they worked to position high-quality instruction as the

Figure 4.1
Linking Quality Teaching and Differentiation

Key Principles Related to the Quality of Student Work in the Classroom

Although many indicators of high-quality curriculum and instruction exist in a classroom, the following eight principles are certainly important on any list. Beneath each of the eight principles indicative of high-quality classrooms is a list of possible indicators of "differentiated instruction"—that is, examples of some of the many ways teachers can ensure that the learning needs of academically diverse learners are met.

1. Curriculum is based on rich and important ideas and skills that help students understand the discipline and practice it in ways similar to experts or professionals in the discipline.
- All students work with rich and important ideas and essential skills, but at levels of difficulty that are appropriately challenging for individuals.
- The teacher uses small-group as well as whole-group instruction to ensure that students understand ideas and skills at an appropriate level of challenge and support.
- The teacher varies the type and amount of scaffolding necessary for a learner to succeed a bit beyond the learner's independence level.

2. Curriculum is relevant and coherent to students, connecting to their lives and helping them understand both their world and the discipline(s) being studied.
- Teachers frequently provide choices of materials, topics, or questions so that students can explore key ideas and use key skills in ways that connect with their own interests.
- A variety of materials is available to deal with key ideas and skills in a broad range of cultures and environments.
- Student products are often shared with audiences meaningful to the student.
- The teacher uses part-to-whole and whole-to-part approaches to help learners understand how each learning experience relates to the larger goals of the unit and year.

3. Teachers and students are clear about and can explain what learners should know, understand, and be able to do as a result of each learning experience.
- Students receive directions in a variety of ways (written, oral, tape-recorded, peer-reviewed) so that each learner understands the goals for the activity or product.
- The teacher uses whole-to-part and part-to-whole approaches that help learners make connections.

4. Instruction, activities, and products clearly focus on key learning goals of the unit of study.
- While students may approach content, activities, and products in different ways, each learner's work focuses on the essential goals of the unit.

5. The lesson interests and engages all learners in the class.
- The teacher varies mode of presentation to reach the range of learning preferences (for example, visual and oral presentations, hands-on as well as print, whole-to-part, and part-to-whole explanations).

(continued)

Figure 4.1—*continued*
Linking Quality Teaching and Differentiation

- Tasks, materials, and products are at appropriate levels of challenge for varying levels of readiness of individuals in the class.
  - Students have choices of how to express their learning.
  - Students help design tasks and products.
  - Students have options for varied modes of working (for example, working alone or with a partner, choice of seating arrangements).
  - When students work collaboratively, tasks are designed so that each student in a group has a contribution to make that is meaningful and important to the success of the group.

6. Activities, discussions, and products call on students to think at high levels and to grapple successfully with complex problems, ideas, issues, and skills.
  - The teacher adjusts question complexity in class discussions to facilitate successful participation by all learners.
  - The teacher uses a variety of discussion formats to maximize student participation and success (for example, Think-Pair-Share, small-group discussions, whole-class discussions, fish bowl, Paideia seminars).
  - Student products address open-ended problems.

7. Students clearly understand criteria for high-quality work in activities and products.
  - Rubrics or lists of criteria for success include elements required for all learners as well as personalized goals at appropriate levels of challenge to ensure student growth.
  - Students contribute to establishing class and personal goals for high-quality work and to determining the degree to which high-quality work is being achieved.
  - Students are assessed both on their own growth and in accordance with agreed-upon norms.

8. The classroom environment is respectful of each student and the group as a whole.
  - Students and teacher work to build a sense of community in which everyone celebrates successes and works together to help overcome obstacles.
  - The teacher helps students to appreciate both their similarities and differences.
  - Teacher and students exhibit genuine caring for one another.
  - The teacher makes continuing efforts to know and understand each student as an individual learner.
  - Varied viewpoints are sought and honored.
  - Each student consistently works in a variety of group and individual settings.
  - The student often makes decisions about how and with whom to work.
  - Students are encouraged to help the teacher find ways to make the work they both do more satisfying.
  - Students actively contribute to making and applying the rules that govern the classroom.
  - The teacher provides varied ways for students to show what they have learned.
  - There is clear evidence of teaching for success.

central concern of all the district did, and differentiation as a necessary part of high-quality instruction. Such documents clarify both thought and planning, and keep the emphasis on quality of curriculum and instruction—where it should always remain.

5. Focus district initiatives. As potential initiatives are proposed for district or school adoption, leaders need to consider their effect on the larger or "umbrella" goal of differentiation. Three steps toward this end are important.

First, determine how important and relevant the potential initiative is in supporting differentiated instruction. Many attractive initiatives do not have a direct and positive effect on creating more responsive classrooms. Those options probably can wait.

Second, think about the initiative from the standpoint of teachers being encouraged to differentiate instruction (or better still, involve them in the decision-making process about potential initiatives). If most teachers are likely to feel overloaded as a result of the proposed initiative, deferring may be wise—or offering teachers who see the initiative as beneficial to their growth in differentiation an *option* to participate.

Third, when new initiatives are adopted, make every effort to ensure that administrators, teachers, staff developers, and parents understand how they contribute to more responsive classrooms. Figure 4.2 shows a graphic used by a district to help teachers reflect on ways in which both new initiatives and those of longer-term emphasis were subsumed under the "umbrella of differentiation." In addition, staff developers must present learning opportunities on new initiatives in such a way that sessions clearly and consistently link with goals of differentiation. Recently, for example, one district planned for extensive teacher training in technology. Because differentiation was a central district goal, virtually all technology workshops were framed to help teachers use technology to address student readiness, interest, and learning profile.

To become more skilled in differentiation, teachers typically have to make significant changes in the ways they think about and carry out instruction. Teaching is already a multitask, multistress endeavor. A meaningful way for administrators to support teachers in differentiation is to limit the number of draws on teacher attention, and to ensure that new demands on their time also help develop and polish the practices of differentiation.

Figure 4.2
Differentiation as an Umbrella for District Initiatives

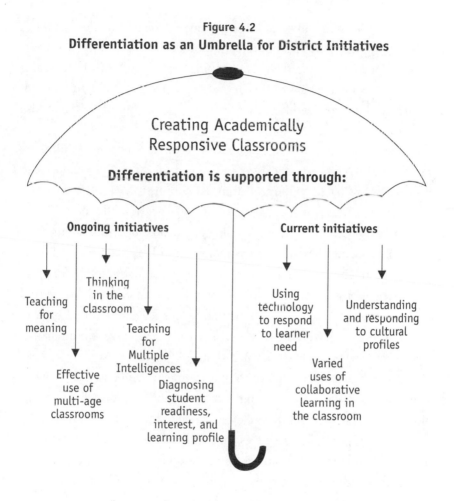

Creating Academically
Responsive Classrooms

Differentiation is supported through:

Ongoing initiatives

Teaching
for
meaning

Thinking
in the
classroom

Teaching
for
Multiple
Intelligences

Effective
use of
multi-age
classrooms

Diagnosing
student
readiness,
interest, and
learning profile

Current initiatives

Using
technology
to respond
to learner
need

Understanding
and responding
to cultural
profiles

Varied
uses of
collaborative
learning in
the classroom

6. Attend to competing mandates. The best efforts of district leaders notwithstanding, mandates or initiatives often appear that "compete" with a goal such as differentiation of instruction. Many times the competing mandate or initiative seems quite powerful to teachers, perhaps because a school board or state-level organization backs it. Educational leaders need to be aware of the effect of such seemingly contradictory messages and to deal with them proactively and positively.

First, realize that the "new" directive may not oppose the goal of responsive instruction, although it may appear that way on the surface. If the two goals truly do not conflict, school administrators should help teachers reconcile the apparent conflict.

A contemporary case in point is the presence in many states of mandated learning standards. Issued from "on high," and backed up with high-stakes testing, the push for standards-based teaching appears blatantly to undermine the teacher's capacity to attend to individual learning differences. Standards and the goal of differentiation, however, ought not to be at odds, for at least two reasons.

First, student learning differences are real. As Susan Ohanian (1999) notes, any teacher who has been in a classroom for even a few minutes is quite clear that students don't all learn the same things according to prescribed time frames—even politically mandated ones. Failure to acknowledge and address variance in readiness, interest, and learning profile does not result in improved learning for academically diverse populations, but rather results in mind-numbing redundancy for some learners and dangerous learning gaps for others. Differentiation suggests that while standards may be set for all learners, the teacher's role is to determine the learning sequences, pace, and degrees of complexity necessary to ensure that each learner truly achieves meaningful standards rather than simply "covering" them.

Second, standards alone do not comprise a meaningful curriculum. They seldom reflect all levels of curriculum (content, process, product, affect, and learning environment), and they seldom attend to all levels of learning (facts, concepts, principles, attitudes, and skills). The teacher's job (along with curriculum specialists) is to weave the standards into more coherent and meaningful frameworks for learning. In those frameworks teachers can hold a standard "steady" for all learners, but vary the materials used to gain information, the activities used to make sense of ideas and apply skills, the modes of expression a student can use in a culminating product, and so on. As Wiggins and McTighe (1998) point out, the teacher's job is to "uncover" the curriculum—not to cover it. Differentiation occurs in the uncovering process. Such an approach does not negate the role of standards, but rather makes more likely the possibility that a full range of students will achieve, retain, and translate the standards into real life.

Standards-based teaching can, but need not, diminish teacher attention to individual learner need. In such high-stakes environments, however, educational leaders need to be proactive in helping teachers reconcile what may appear to be contradictory directions.

Because differentiation is rooted in best-practice teaching, few well-conceived directives or initiatives focused on the classroom should be in conflict with the principles and goals of creating responsive classrooms. If such instances occur, however, effective leadership provides teachers a chance to talk about the contradictions, the stresses they create, and the means of handling those stresses in the most effective ways possible.

An example of responding to these stresses occurred in a district with rapid growth, where double-session classes were necessary for a year in a number of schools. Doubling up on school use was unavoidable, and the greatly shortened school day obviously made it far more difficult for teachers to know students well, plan fluid instruction, and even to make optimal use of school materials and facilities. In this setting, district leaders, principals, and teachers openly discussed the negative effect of double sessions on their goals of differentiation. They also planned for creative ways to minimize the effect of the unavoidable scheduling problems on attending to the needs of varied learners. One solution teachers used was to create student profile folders in the spring prior to the double-session year. Teachers and students worked together to contribute to a folder for each learner that indicated special interests, ways in which the student learned best, strengths and weaknesses in key subject areas, and relevant test data. Teachers for the upcoming year could pick up folders at the school for students who were assigned to their classes in the double-session year—during the summer, if possible, as soon as the schedules were complete.

Teaching is demanding and complex at best. Wise leaders who envision more responsive classrooms at district and school levels support teachers in differentiation by doing whatever they can to keep teachers from feeling unnecessarily pulled in multiple directions at once.

7. Plan for leadership and support. To our knowledge, no one has ever wished responsive classrooms into reality—or even commanded them into being. In the early stages of planning systemic movement toward differentiation, system leaders should construct a plan that addresses the need to have day-to-day leaders for the effort, as well as classroom-level support. These factors are essential for widespread change.

Administrative support at all levels for differentiation is a nonnegotiable item for systemic change. While district-level leaders are especially effective in commending differentiation, establishing policies that support differentiation, and celebrating accomplishments in differentiating, school-level leaders are the linchpins of daily implementation. The principal is physically present in the school on a day-to-day basis. As a result, she has the capacity to make differentiation a consistent expectation, support and commend teacher growth toward more effective differentiation, and monitor progress in developing effectively differentiated classrooms. The principal is also closer to the daily problems in the school and classroom, and therefore better able to anticipate problems and propose solutions. Further, the principal is key in helping district leaders understand and target the sorts of support teachers need in their growth toward differentiation that can be provided only from the district level. Principals must be a part of defining the need and developing the vision for differentiation as well as defining roles of various school personnel in fostering differentiation at the school level. In addition to administrative leadership, teachers need support at the classroom level as well if they are to make major changes in their practice. Most districts hire specialists in learning disabilities, reading proficiency, gifted education, teaching English as a second language, and so on. Often, however, the work of such experts is largely, or even wholly, separated from the work of the general classroom teacher.

To make effective differentiation a reality, new partnerships are needed among specialists and generalists. These partnerships do not happen easily. The culture of teaching is characterized by isolation. We often do not know how to talk to one another, how to solve problems together, or how to share turf.

No classroom teacher can have specialized knowledge that benefits every type of student: those with learning disabilities, those for whom English is a second language, students from a wide spectrum of cultures, learners who are volatile, those who learn with lightning speed or at great depths of understanding, and a range of other specific needs. Likewise, no specialist can fully know all areas of curriculum. Classroom teacher–specialist collaborations are essential.

To maximize the shared efforts of general classroom teachers and specialists, leaders for effective differentiation should consider the following suggestions:

• Ensure large blocks of time in the specialist's schedule for direct collaboration with classroom teachers in the regular classroom.

• Encourage each specialist to develop a few in-depth collaborations in a given year rather than only flitting in and out of many classrooms.

• Provide guided planning and problem solving time, throughout a year or more, in which collaborators are given assistance (for example, by district coordinators of gifted education, district language arts specialists, department chairs, etc.) in developing a shared understanding of differentiation, identifying needs of specific learners, clarifying instructional goals, evolving instructional plans, evaluating both teacher and student progress, and working out roles for each teacher.

• Change the perception of "ownership" of a certain category of students to a sense of shared responsibility for all students (so that, for instance, the specialist in learning disabilities contributes specialized knowledge in ways that would benefit students with learning disabilities, but also in ways that would benefit a wider range of learners; and so that the learning-disabilities specialist works with mixed-readiness groups, advanced learners, or interest-based groups—as well as with learning-disabled students—in the general classroom).

• Help both specialists and classroom teachers become comfortable with the idea that not having all the answers is okay, and to accept the goal of learning together—through successes and glitches—to develop an effective differentiated classroom.

• Encourage effective collaborative teams to serve as models for other collaborative teams as they form over time (through guidance from earlier teams on how to facilitate and support the teaming process, videotaping planning sessions or classroom lessons, team-led staff development, formal sharing of written lessons and lesson materials, and observations in the collaborative classroom).

• Encourage collaborative teams of classroom teachers and specialists to propose options for their own professional development in differentiation, as well as contributing to professional-development options for colleagues.

• Recognize both publicly and privately the risks, efforts, and successes of collaborative teams.

Effective differentiation cannot have as its goal the elimination of specialists.

The need for specialized knowledge in classrooms has never been greater. Rather, a goal of differentiation is focusing more of the specialist's time in the regular classroom and doing so more effectively than in the past.

Likewise, eliminating all special services outside the regular classroom is not a goal of differentiation. For some students, learning needs are so extreme (whether in regard to difficulty with learning, advancement in learning, emotional volatility, or other profile) that they cannot be adequately addressed in the general classroom. The goal of differentiation is to maximize the capacity of the general classroom to serve appropriately a wide and diverse range of learners. As we grow in that capacity, the degree to which we will need out-of-classroom services should diminish, though not disappear.

8. Allocate financial resources. Few things in education are readily accomplished without financial resources. While recognizing that money cannot replace motivation and energy, you must assess the resources available to you and develop your expectations and timelines accordingly. Enthusiasm is dampened when leaders overpromise and underdeliver. When we ask much of teachers, we must be ready to support them with expert guidance, time to collaborate and plan, high-quality staff development, materials, and other supports that inevitably carry a price tag. Our commitment to change is made clear when we invest in what we want.

9. Look ahead to assessing progress. From the earliest stages of movement toward systemic change, leaders should have a plan to determine what is working and what needs modification. A clear statement of philosophy or vision as well as goals at the front end of planning provide a measuring rod for assessing progress all along the journey. Early on, ask and answer questions such as: *Where do we want to go? What steps do we follow to get there? When do we take stock of our progress? How do we get assistance to conduct meaningful and useful evaluations of our growth? What do we do with what we learn in assessments?* Many educational initiatives are stillborn because no one drew a roadmap for growth, nor a viable plan for learning from our journey, nor a systematic way of turning experience into progress.

10. Plan for the long haul. Making differentiation a centerpiece of district plans is important. Leaders should focus even more, however, on making clear that the effort to develop more effectively differentiated classrooms will remain at the core of district planning for a long time to come. Helping teachers change their practice in significant ways takes a long time. A one- or two-year commitment to differentiation falls far short of what is required for major change. Further, when a school or district pattern of initiatives flickers in and out of vogue, teachers quickly learn they can bide their time and excuse themselves of a need to grapple with change.

Actually, as long as student populations are academically diverse, learning to address that diversity ought to be a central factor in hiring teachers and administrators, planning for their professional growth, and assessing their effectiveness. In essence, people systemwide should understand that the quest to be more effective with academically diverse populations will not "go away." To develop an effective cadre of distinguished teachers requires that growth toward differentiation be at the forefront of district concern and planning from now on. Some useful ways to clarify the ongoing importance of differentiation in schools and districts are as follows:

• Disseminate print or Web site materials that explain the goals of differentiation, provide a rationale for it, define it, and indicate a high degree of ongoing support for it.

• Develop long-term district plans for supporting differentiated instruction (minimum of seven to ten years into the future).

• Develop short-term district, school, and teacher goals for increasing classroom responsiveness to academic diversity (semester or year-long goals).

• Spell out the role differentiation plays in growth of teachers and administrators toward professional expertise.

• Clarify ways in which differentiation helps students achieve benchmarks and standards.

The Best Laid Plans

School change is complex, unpredictable, and messy. No one has come up with a failsafe plan for it. Nonetheless, clarity of purpose, mutual vision, and wise first steps can make a significant difference in team building, efficient use of resources, and reduction of tension as the change effort moves into the implementation stage.

One additional reminder to smooth the way for growth: Models of effective differentiation—pieces of the vision at work—are already in place in every school or district. Be sure to look around carefully for those people and practices you should spotlight, learn from, and use as a platform for progress. Everyone likes to know you're not really starting from scratch.

rsonnel, strategies that lend concrete support for differentiation, strate-
o promote sharing of ideas, and structural strategies that aid in differ-
tion. Because of the central role of effective staff development in
mic change, Chapter 6 addresses that category of implementation
egies separately and at greater length.

ategies That Focus on Personnel

ull understanding of differentiation implies a school full of educators and
dents working together to create a community in which everyone is
couraged to become the very best they can be. In such places, every adult
s a key role to play. Differentiation is not just the job of the classroom
cher. In Chapter 4, we highlighted the importance of early planning for
sroom teacher/specialist partnerships. Beyond those collaborations, how-
districts or schools wanting to multiply the success of differentiation
e roles for many other categories of personnel also as they move from
on of a change plan to its implementation.

for Differentiation

districts focus hiring on the goals of differentiation, seeking new
ho have skills in planning and directing multitask classrooms, or
o clearly have the capacity and willingness to develop those
stricts focus considerable staff development for new teachers on
practices of differentiation. Districts then pair the new teach-
ues more experienced in differentiation to help with transfer
lerstanding from staff development into classroom practice.
promise exists for fostering differentiation skills in teachers
ct with a clear understanding and acceptance of differen-
otiable district initiative.

Specialists

media specialist made it a point to talk with each
g materials over the summer. He ensured that he con-
g collection of materials at a wide range of difficulty
s and concepts were central to teachers' instruction.
used a rich store of materials of different sorts that

Practical Strategies for Implementing a Differentiation Growth Plan

Once leaders develop a coherent plan to begin helping p
a district grow in their capacity to address varied lea
concrete and practical strategies can be quite help
the plan. The strategies draw on key principles of effecti
tiation and address the daily actions of all educators ir
These strategies also, of necessity, are situation spec
account the needs of individuals, schools, and the
strategies are most likely to result in positive ch
Any given school or district would probably r
gies equally useful, or even appropriate to a
thoughtful use of a number of the strateg
encouragement, credibility, and suppor
number of classrooms that are more

In fact, each of the implementa
has been used to positive advan
ously tried to promote differer
on varied sets of these impl
Sheridan, Colorado; Bois
County, Maryland; An
Hill, North Carolina:
ton, Oregon; Alber
ville, Virginia; M
Calgary and Ed
tories, Canada.

Though teachers can u
this chapter organizes and discu

Hiring

Many
teachers
teachers w
skills. The d
principles and
ers with collea
of skills and un
Great long-term
who enter a distr
tiation as a nonne

Involving Media

In one school, the
teacher before orderin
tinued to build a growi
levels on whatever topic
Over time, this library ho

greatly enhanced differentiation efforts in all subjects at all grades.

Another media specialist struggled with how to be more effective when individuals and small groups came to the library to do differentiated tasks requiring media center resources. She developed a form that students completed before leaving their classrooms, stating the nature of their task and goals for the day. The classroom teacher read and approved the forms before students left the room. On entering the library, students presented their forms to the media specialist, who was then quickly able to help students access materials and focus on the task at hand. Before leaving the library, students completed another section of the form in which they described what they had accomplished, how they had worked, and (if appropriate) their next goals or tasks in completing their assignment. The media specialist approved or revised the form that students then took to their classroom teacher. Everyone felt more secure, and the quality of student work increased dramatically.

Calling on Skills of Guidance Counselors

In one school, the guidance counselor observed and helped out in classrooms in order to spot students who lacked the social and emotional skills necessary to work successfully in groups. She then formed miniclasses of such students from across grade levels or classes and worked with them to develop group skills. She also provided suggestions to teachers of ways they might promote the success of these students in groups, and of groups in general. The counselor continued to work in classes periodically to spot new problem areas, reinforce successes of students who were improving in group skills, refine the content of her miniclasses, and come to know the school's students better in their roles as learners.

Enlisting Technology Specialists to Assist with Differentiation

Numerous districts closely link the role of technology specialists with differentiation efforts, ensuring that technology is a central tool in differentiation, that software and Internet use are targeted to particular student interests and needs, and that technology specialists are central in helping teachers plan for differentiated curriculum and instruction. Staff development conducted by technology specialists focuses on technology as a means for addressing learner variance. One district developed a cadre of classroom teachers who were already comfortable using technology in their classrooms and provided extended learning opportunities for this group on how to use technology to differentiate instruction. The work of these teachers subsequently provided concrete and highly relevant examples of the link at the classroom level between technology and differentiation that could be shared with peers in their schools and across the district.

Using Social Workers in Difficult Settings

In one district, school social workers played an essential role in working side by side with teachers in classrooms that had a significant number of volatile learners. The social worker sat with small groups of students, coaching them for individual and group success. He sometimes removed students from the classroom briefly to prevent outbursts, working with a student until that student was ready to return to the classroom successfully. In this particular setting, the importance of the social worker's role is paramount in allowing differentiation to take place in these complex classrooms.

Recruiting Retirees to Coach for Differentiation

When teachers retire from a school or district, they often take immense expertise with them. While they may be looking forward to retirement, many retirees are happy to contribute on a periodic basis to the continued growth of other educators in the district. One district carefully selected retirees who had demonstrated the skills of differentiation in their classrooms. These former teachers served as differentiation coaches in a number of ways—sometimes offering practical staff development, sometimes assisting with planning sessions, and often in a teacher's classroom to lend a hand with small-group instruction or aiding with early management concerns.

Strategies That Lend Concrete Support for Differentiation

Too often we ask teachers to do something complex and expend extra effort with little thought about what leaders should do to make the effort more attractive. The intent of incentives is not to "pay" teachers for being professionals (in other words, for continued learning, for refining expertise, for addressing the needs of their clients, and so on). Rather, such incentives are symbolic ways of offering partnership in an endeavor valued by the district.

Providing Opportunities to See Differentiation in Action

Most teachers likely have no images of what a differentiated classroom would look like. Teachers who are charged with developing such classrooms need to see how differentiation looks for their grade level and subject matter. Several school districts have hired a professional videographer to make brief, but high-quality, videotapes of teachers' classrooms where differentiation is taking place within the district. Not only can such tapes, especially if narrated effectively, provide missing images of differentiation but they can also send the key message that differentiation happens in "my" district and with students like "mine."

Two neighboring and similar districts formed an exchange program in which a teacher from one district could visit in the nearby district a grade or class where differentiation was taking place. Shared staff development allowed for periodic debriefing about observations, as did less formal exchanges between teachers before, during, or after visits.

Making Multitext Adoptions

In one district, student readiness levels in social studies classes varied a great deal. To ensure that teachers have important resources to undertake differentiation in those classes, the district used multitext adoption rather than the typical single-text approach. Within a given social studies class, then, two or more texts on the same topics (for example, American History) might be available, but with quite a range of readability levels. Having texts appropriate for the full range of learners can prove quite a boost to a teacher's early efforts at differentiation.

Offering Minigrants

Developing differentiated classrooms often implies the need for materials at different reading levels or based on differing student interests. Basic materials needed for effective differentiation such as texts, manipulatives, lab materials, and so on are the responsibility of the school or district, of course. Beyond that, however, many differentiated units are richer with a variety of supplementary materials. Teachers should not have to scrounge for or purchase such materials themselves. One district established a Differentiation Minigrant Program to enable teachers to secure funding for supplementary materials that would enhance the quality of differentiated units. Figure 5.1 shows the short application teachers completed to request funds. Its purpose was to ensure that a teacher had a specific plan to use the materials for differentiation. Grants were awarded up to $150. Virtually all applicants were funded.

Supporting Conference Attendance

Despite tight budgets, several districts routinely set aside funding for some teachers to attend conferences and institutes that augment the evolving knowledge about differentiation. District leaders match the conference with teacher need or level of expertise. Sending "early subscribers" to conferences or institutes that support them in becoming effective leaders of differentiation is particularly useful. Attendance at a state, regional, or national

---

Figure 5.1
Differentiation Minigrant Application

Name of Teacher: _____

School and Grade Level/Subject: _____

• The project that I'd like to do:

• The learning needs of students in my classroom that I want to address:

• How I plan to differentiate the instruction:

• What I'll need and a proposed budget:

Source: From the Grosse Pointe, Michigan, Public School System, 1999. Reproduced by permission.

---

conference with an emphasis on differentiation can also enhance or renew the energy of less skilled teachers.

One district offered a number of conference scholarships annually for school teams to attend high-quality conferences that supported differentiation. Teams are composed of classroom teachers, specialists, and at least one administrator. Interested teams applied for the scholarships by stating their goals for growth in differentiation, explaining how the particular conference would likely help them achieve the goals, and explaining concrete contributions that would result (such as sharing differentiated curriculum, offering staff development sessions, creating a mininewsletter to share insights about differentiation from the conference, and so on). The district typically supported four to six such teams a year in conference attendance, taking care to nurture the growth of the team when they returned.

Providing Recognition for Teacher Efforts and Growth

Several districts have literally celebrated educator contributions toward differentiating instruction. One school's parent organization hosted "birthday" celebrations at the point each year that marked the anniversary of the school's inauguration of differentiated classrooms. Held instead of a monthly faculty meeting, the celebration provided good refreshments, decorations, and a chance for parents to share with teachers what differentiation means for their children. Needless to say, the sharing was most powerful. Another district held a "reunion" for teachers who had studied differentiation over several summers. The surroundings and the refreshments were elegant. Most important, however, was the chance teachers had to reconnect with like-minded peers and the opportunity for the group to give district leaders guidance on next steps in the district's growth in differentiating instruction.

Still another district asked local businesses that were school partners to host an annual banquet for teachers who had contributed to the district's growth in differentiation over the previous year. The large number of teachers attending had shared differentiated lessons for district distribution, contributed to staff development in differentiation, served as peer partners in differentiation, invited others to observe in their classrooms, served on curriculum planning teams, and so on.

Strategies That Promote Sharing of Ideas

Teaching is often a lonely profession. One teacher can do something wonderful in her classroom and the teacher two doors down the hall has no idea that anything happened. Four teachers in the same building may create materials on a given topic, never knowing about the duplication of effort among them. Because good differentiation is labor intensive on the part of teachers, linking their efforts is an important way to promote sharing and save time. This type of sharing also is likely to increase teacher understanding of differentiation rather than simply "copying" what someone else did. Schools and districts serious about differentiation seek ways to multiply teacher effectiveness and time by ensuring dissemination and informed sharing of teacher efforts.

Using Core Groups to Spread the Word

A number of districts have carefully selected core groups of teachers (generally no more than 10) who agree to pioneer the effort to understand and implement differentiation. Multiple core groups may be used in large districts. Districts provide time and leadership for these teachers to develop a sound framework of understanding of differentiation, to work together to develop differentiated lessons, to share what they are doing with principals, and ultimately to serve as catalysts for their colleagues' growth. Along the way, core groups may share examples of differentiated lessons (on paper or in faculty discussions), answer teacher questions, and help develop printed materials about differentiation for colleagues to use. Heavy initial investment in such groups has repeatedly proven to be powerful and effective in many districts. Most districts have discovered that at the end of a year, the previous group is ready to provide leadership for subsequent groups, but also has a strong desire to remain together for continued growth themselves. This desire demonstrates the complexity of learning to differentiate instruction. Providing ongoing support groups of more experienced teachers while initiating study groups of less experienced ones is a wise investment of time and leadership.

One district developed catalyst study groups specifically composed of classroom teachers, gifted-education specialists, special educators, and reading teachers. These groups not only formed a common understanding of the processes and practices of differentiation but also worked together in the study groups as well as in the classrooms to evolve roles and guidelines for effective classroom collaboration. This early pioneering by specialists made later partnerships with classroom teachers far smoother and better focused.

Using Shared Reflective Journals

In one middle school, the principal encouraged his teachers to keep journals, or even informal jottings, of observations about their individual students and their learning profiles. He also kept a journal, noting insights from classroom visits, cafeteria and bus duty, and conversations with students in his office. The journals became a shared vehicle for attending to students as individuals, focusing on learner responses to a variety of learning experiences, and faculty conversations about the student population they served. Journals helped these educators "see" their students better and reflect more effectively on what was and wasn't working in the classroom for various learners.

Creating Curriculum Tubs

One district brought together teams of teachers at a given grade level or subject area across schools. The teams had time during the school year and later in the summer to agree on concepts around which they could teach required state standards. After creating teaching outlines that delineated concepts, topics, and skills keyed to each unit and directly to state standards, teachers brought in materials and activities that supported the learning goals. The teams worked together to organize the activities and materials, and then to differentiate lessons based on the goals and materials. Ultimately the groups of teachers created a curriculum tub for each unit, placing in a large plastic tub or bin (with a lid) teaching outlines keyed to state standards, possible differentiated lessons, and materials that supported the unit in general as well as the differentiation. When necessary, the district helped create multiple tubs for one unit to aid in dissemination. Teachers could check out tubs from a district media center, keeping them in their classrooms for the duration of the unit. Teachers were also asked to add at least one new idea or piece of material to the tub before returning it at the end of the unit.

Using Mailbox Staff Development

A secondary school found many teachers hesitant to subscribe to the need for differentiation. A group of teachers who used differentiated instruction effectively and who accepted leadership responsibility developed clever flyers or brief newsletters that were placed in teacher mailboxes or in teachers' lounges from time to time. In this format, they shared their experiences with differentiation (both positive and negative), reflected on why it seemed worth the effort, and most importantly, included student responses to their efforts. While the publications did not change everyone's mind, they were very effective at starting discussions and in increasing interest and participation by some "fence sitters."

Providing Effective Materials as Lures to Learning

In one district, a determined staff developer whose district lacked a coherent plan for differentiation effectively used core groups to develop a base of interest and expertise in differentiation. She increased the circle of interest by offering staff development carefully targeted, key facets of differentiated instruction. She also made attendance at the optional sessions interesting to teachers by providing high-quality materials on differentiation to whoever attended the sessions. Sometimes she provided "how-to" handouts (for example, how to differentiate a science lab, or strategies for supporting reading in a mixed-readiness classroom). At other times she provided published materials on differentiation or distributed copies of lessons that had been differentiated and proved effective in classroom use. Attendance at the staff development sessions remained high over a period of more than two years, certainly because the sessions themselves were useful, but also because the teachers thought the "freebies" were great!

Structural Strategies That Aid Differentiation

Leaders can initiate a number of structural changes in schools that enable teachers to be more responsive to learner needs. Such changes are beyond the capacity of the teacher and are certainly systemic in nature. These approaches, which affect allocation of time and arrangement of students, are particularly powerful "levers" in providing momentum for differentiation.

Developing Multi-age Classrooms

When students of several grade levels are in one classroom, the need to differentiate becomes paramount. A philosophy of responsiveness comes with the territory. One district encouraged teachers at primary, elementary, and middle-school levels to form multi-age groupings in each grade configuration. They were staffed by teachers who elected to work in these complex but flexible settings. The work of these teachers pioneered for the district in developing differentiated curriculum, managing multitask classrooms, communicating with parents, and assessing the effectiveness of differentiated approaches for students and teachers alike.

Promoting Looping

Looping is the practice of teachers working with the same students for more than one year. Teachers "loop" or "move up" with students when they progress to the next grade. This approach to teaching helps teachers and students know one another much better, saves much of the "starting over" time when students and teachers are new to each other every year, helps build a much greater sense of community among students, and promotes relationships between teacher and parents. One district also focused on looping as a way to justify teachers' time to find out about their students in order to differentiate instruction. In this instance, teachers developed student profile portfolios, parent-teacher communication strategies, and even interest-based summer activities—none of which would have been likely to occur in more typical single-year relationships between students and their teacher.

Assigning Clusters of Students

Cluster grouping places purposeful groups of students (generally on the order of three to eight students) with similar learning needs in an otherwise mixed-ability classroom. Cluster groups give teachers a critical mass of like learners for planning and targeting instruction. For many teachers, especially in the early stages of learning to differentiate instruction, clusters are preferable to "teaching in Noah's Ark," where the teacher has two of every kind of student in the school. Cluster groups can help teachers feel less scattered in their thinking and teaching. (Cluster grouping should be only one facet of a differentiated classroom, with all students working with the widest possible variety of students in the classroom at appropriate times.) One district clustered students of similar learning needs in classes of volunteer teachers and supported the work of these teachers by assigning specialists to those classrooms for up to two hours/periods per day. For example, a teacher with a cluster of students for whom English was not their first language would have the assistance of the ESL teacher directly in their classrooms each day. Sometimes the specialist may work directly with the cluster students, but often she is simply a second pair of hands and eyes, working collaboratively to make the classroom better for many students—and offering special guidance on working with the cluster students as well.

Creating Learning Centers to Support a Range of Learners

To improve the logistics of teachers creating small groups with differentiated tasks, have an alternative place for students to work with supervision and guidance at key times. While this systemic strategy carries a price tag, a center that is staffed by paraprofessionals or even volunteers working under a teacher's direction has lower expenses. In one district, such a center was used effectively for advanced learners working on independent studies, students having difficulty with a particular skill or concept, students with extended absences, individuals or small groups needing guidance on product development, and so on.

Add to the List of Strategies

We hope you find some of these strategies useful in implementing a differentiation plan in your school or district. Take time, too, however, to work with classroom teachers, specialists, administrators, and other school personnel to develop your own list of strategies to both lure and support educators in the process of learning about and implementing differentiation. Draw on your staff's creativity, their understanding of the needs and culture of the schools and district, and be sure the strategies you develop are responsive to the readiness levels, interests, and learning profiles of teachers in your district. Strategies that derive from teacher need, insight, and experience are likely to be powerful and to demonstrate support for teachers in a difficult (and rewarding) job.

Staff Development That Supports Differentiation

F rank, a respected middle school social studies teacher within a year of
retirement, stands in the hall outside of his classroom and booms to
his assistant principal, "This differentiated instruction is difficult, frustrating, and time consuming—and I would *never* go back to teaching the old way!" What forces came into play that would cause an experienced and very successful teacher nearing the end of his career to invest substantial energy in significantly revising his instructional behavior and strategies? Frank was a faculty member in a school system undergoing a districtwide initiative asking all teachers to differentiate classroom instruction. Intensive staff development, which was a cornerstone of the district effort, contributed significantly to both his skill and will related to differentiating instruction.

In moving toward more effectively differentiated classrooms, staff development spans the initiation, implementation, and continuation phases of change. Development of staff must be a part of early planning, needs to be refined as teachers develop greater expertise, and should remain central to any attempts to address academic diversity as long as the students with varying needs continue to show us that one-size-fits-all is a poor fit for many. Staff development is so essential that it merits separate and extended consideration.

In this chapter, we first briefly examine evidence for the central role of staff development in movement toward differentiation; then make specific suggestions for the nature of staff development related to differentiation; and finally propose a sequence of topics, types of understanding, and skills that are likely to be important to teachers at various stages of proficiency with classroom implementation.

The Importance of Staff Development in Movement Toward Differentiation

Staff development is a regularly underestimated component of educational improvement. In the ongoing struggle to adequately fund education, budgets are often slashed in categories related to development of our teachers and administrators. This development is particularly ironic as American business and industry become increasingly aware of the need to invest in human resources to remain effective in the face of competition and change. The urgency of effective staff development for schools that intend to succeed is a keystone of the national report, *Doing What Matters Most: Investing in Quality Teaching* (Darling-Hammond, 1997).

> After a decade of reform, we have finally learned in hindsight what should have been clear from the start: Most schools and teachers cannot produce the kind of learning demanded by the new reforms—not because they do not want to, but because they do not know how, and the systems in which they work do not support them in doing so (p. 8).

The power of staff development to support educators in making change is likely greater than we have acknowledged. For example, studies tell us that teachers who know a great deal about teaching and learning and who work in environments that allow them to know students well are a very powerful factor in determining student achievement—a far more powerful determinant than class size. Further, expenditures for securing and developing teacher expertise are more potent than other less instructionally targeted spending (Ferguson, 1991).

In regard to educator readiness to address academic diversity, indications are that we have a great distance to go in building proficiency, let alone expertise. For example, teachers appear to make few modifications to benefit students in their classes with particular learning needs, whether those students struggle or are advanced (Archambault et al., 1993; McIntosh, Vaughn, Schumm, Haager, & Lee, 1993). Further, veteran teachers appear to use few instructional strategies that invite looking at students in small groups and as individuals, as compared to addressing them as a whole (Moon, Tomlinson, & Callahan, 1995). In addition, novice teachers appear to enter the ranks of teaching with little knowledge of how to address academic diversity and little encouragement to do so (Tomlinson et al., 1995).

What we see here is the power of effective staff development (coupled with encouraging school environments) to change teacher practice in desirable ways. In a time when school populations are steadily, if not exponentially, becoming more academically diverse, few teachers seem to effectively address the needs of their academically diverse classrooms. Indications are that without considerably greater expertise in effective teaching of academically diverse populations, our schools will fail many young people whose education is entrusted to us. Implications for high-quality staff development in differentiating instruction are clear.

> Changing times require that schools become learning enterprises for teachers and for students. The way teachers currently learn on the job was designed for teachers of an earlier time before the public grew concerned with higher standards and improved performance for all students. . . . Today's teachers must take on new roles within the school and be able to teach young people from diverse backgrounds by drawing on a large repertoire of subject matter and teaching skills (National Foundation for the Improvement of Education, 1996, preface).

Characteristics of Effective Staff Development on Differentiation

When planning for staff development that changes classroom practice, leaders should examine staff development efforts that have proven effective in fostering effective differentiation (see the following sections). Leaders should draw on their own knowledge and experience related to staff development that is worthy of teachers' time and the trust placed in us by students and their families.

Staff Development Should Be Built on a Common Vocabulary Related to Differentiation

If a district or a school is to seriously infuse differentiated instruction into the classroom, all teachers need to have the same basic vocabulary and core understanding. In the same way that a teacher may present introductory material to a whole class, a district or school needs to be able to present and build on a common set of material and concepts to be understood. Beyond introductory phases, other staff development should continue to use and build on the same vocabulary and principles.

Staff Development Should Attend to Teachers' Levels of Readiness (Information, Comprehension, Skills, Commitment), Interest, and Preferred Learning Modes

Teachers should have opportunities to participate in staff development of their own selection that is geared to their particular needs. Staff development should address teachers' current comfort levels with differentiation. Activities within those offerings ideally would provide for multiple learning profiles and differing ways of accessing similar material. Even within introductory activities that use nondifferentiated content, alternative learning activities can be provided. For example, a half-day introductory workshop for new teachers simply provided both an observation of a video and a reading-and-discussion group geared to the same learning objective and asked the participants to join the group that they felt was the best suited to their personal learning style. To differentiate staff development is to practice what we preach.

Staff Development Should Offer Options Directly Focused on Particular Needs of Particular Grade Levels and Subject Areas

Staff development should accommodate the needs and perceptions of both primary grade and high school teachers. Although the principles of differentiation are generalizable, and many of the strategies work across grade-level and subject areas, teachers benefit from staff development that is tailored to their grade level or subject area. Specificity of models and examples helps bring classroom practice to life, helps teachers identify their own questions and needs, and encourages implementation. Staff development is also more effective when designed around the reality that some teachers need greater assistance with planning for differentiated instruction, some with managing differentiated classrooms, and many with both elements simultaneously.

Staff Development Plans Must Include School Administrators and Other District Leaders Who Will Work with Teachers

Leaders must increase their own expertise to be able to support and assess teachers' growth. Leaders must have an understanding of the district's vocabulary of differentiation, what differentiation looks like in the classroom, and the process by which teachers might develop their skills. Dialogues between administrative leaders and teachers should be ongoing so that administrators develop an understanding of both the growth and continuing struggles of teachers who seek to teach academically diverse populations. This understanding is essential for administrative leaders who want to provide effectively targeted assessment of progress and support. Such an understanding is also critical for support personnel such as media specialists, technology specialists, guidance counselors, and social workers who can—if appropriately prepared—be important facilitators of more effective differentiation.

Staff Development on Differentiation Should Consistently Emphasize High-Quality Curriculum and Instruction as the Starting Point for Meaningful Differentiation

The toughest challenge in education is ensuring that student work in each classroom is rich, important, and meaningful. We need to stress continually what best-practice curriculum and instruction look like, and then help teachers learn to differentiate it. Differentiation as a magic potion loses much, if not most, of its power if what we differentiate is mediocre in quality. Staff development should always make the point that we begin with high-quality student work and then differentiate it.

Staff Development Should Be Planned To Ensure Transfer of Knowledge, Understanding, and Skill into the Classroom

Staff development should consistently ask teachers to plan to use what they are learning in their classrooms, assess the effectiveness of what they implemented, and select new learning opportunities based on logical next steps in their own growth. Staff development that is designed for transfer also provides opportunities and encouragement for teachers to collaborate in all of these phases. Study groups, peer coaching, coteaching, guided curriculum development, and guided observations may be among the effective forms of staff development in this regard.

Staff Development Offered by the School or District Should Be Consistent and Aligned with District Differentiation Goals

All staff development offered by the district or school should help teachers learn new ways to attend to student needs, see additional examples of how differentiation might be enacted in a classroom, and understand its connection with high-quality instruction. A helpful approach to staff development on technology, for example, is to stress ways in which technology can be an effective tool for dealing with ranges of student readiness, interest, and learning profile. In contrast, teachers are in a difficult position if district- or school-level staff development suggests only one formula for teaching all students to read, one way to use graphic organizers, one effective mode of cooperative learning, and so on.

Staff Development That Asks Much of Teachers Must Recognize Teacher Efforts

When teachers are asked to make a major commitment to change, the school or district should demonstrate its own commitment by providing support to teachers in the form of payment for beyond-school hours spent in staff development, released time for creation of differentiated curriculum, recognition programs, tuition reimbursement for related coursework, and so on.

The Content of Staff Development on Differentiation

If we honor the premise that teachers would benefit from differentiation exactly as their students would, we should approach staff development in terms of varied levels of complexity, based both on varying teacher proficiency and the school's or district's evolution in moving toward more effectively differentiated classrooms.

While the levels of staff development suggested here are somewhat artificial, you should keep in mind the sorts of information, concepts, and skills that educators need to develop as they progress in their understanding and application of differentiation. Remember that educators reside at each level of development, and that each topic discussed in the following sections can be explored at varied levels of complexity. Remember, too, that teachers themselves are valuable sources of topics and conditions for staff development. [Three matrixes or checklists included in the Appendix (Figures A.1, A.2, and A.3) may be useful to teachers at varied levels of proficiency or with varying professional development goals in diagnosing their own learning needs related to differentiation, planning differentiated classrooms, and reflecting on their differentiated teaching.]

Basic-Level Staff Development

The basic level of staff development needs to involve all staff members in a school or district to at least some degree to ensure a common understanding of district or school goals for differentiation and shared vocabulary and principles related to differentiation. Beyond that initial exposure, some teachers are likely to need additional work with the rudiments of differentiation, while others may have already progressed to a more complex understanding and application of it.

Experiences at this level are introductory. Methods of content delivery are likely to take the form of presentations, hands-on workshops, videos, readings, and discussion groups. Where possible, classroom visitations are useful at this stage. Staff development can also prepare teachers to begin immediately to apply in their classroom the concepts and skills they learn through staff development. Coaching and consultation should be a part of many basic-level staff development options. Approaches to basic-level staff development and activities to support them include

• Awareness of the need for differentiation—including the rationale and evidence that supports the need to differentiate instruction.

• Identifying key vocabulary, features, concepts, and principles of differentiated instruction.

• Identifying and applying some basic instructional strategies that are currently employed in the teacher's classroom and ways in which those strategies might be used most effectively for differentiation.

• Effective use of multiple teacher presentation modes and multiple student materials.

• Introducing and applying other basic instructional strategies that invite differentiation (for example: reading buddies, varying writing prompts, varying questions, and so on).

- Creating "respectful" tasks.
- Differentiating according to one student trait (readiness, interest, or learning profile).
- Using instructional strategies to meet key learning goals and to build student engagement and understanding.
- Planning for whole-group vs. small-group or individual work.
- Developing specific guidelines for implementing the targeted approaches to differentiation so that the teacher has a comfortable plan for managing basic differentiated classroom routines (giving directions, monitoring group functioning, starting and stopping group tasks, setting expectations for student behavior, plans for students who finish work early, etc.).

Staff Development at Mid-Level Proficiency

As teachers develop a sense of comfort and competence with the rudiments of planning for and managing a multitask classroom, staff development should begin to deal with somewhat more complex issues and approaches. Guided work times with hands-on application are especially useful at this point. Additional readings on topics relevant to teacher need and interest, ongoing classroom visits, and consultation with specialists in varying areas of student need can also be powerful. Among topics that may serve as the focus of mid-level staff development on differentiation are

- Student assessment: diagnosing student readiness, interest, and learning profiles and assessing student progress.
- Consistent use of assessment as a catalyst for instructional planning.
- Planning high-quality instruction as a baseline for differentiation.
- Classroom management strategies: establishing student expectations, managing groups in the classroom, preparing students for ongoing differentiation, keeping track of student progress.
- Purposeful planning for flexible grouping.
- Balancing teacher-choice and student-choice options.
- Using a variety of specific instructional strategies to differentiate content, process, and product.
- Understanding and planning instruction responsive to cultures.
- Differentiating by readiness, interest, and learning profile in a single learning experience or within a brief sequence of lessons.

• Establishing clarity about what students should know, understand, and be able to do as a result of a given lesson, lesson sequence, and unit.
  • Creating a classroom environment that supports learner differences.
  • Helping students become more self-reliant learners.
  • Communicating with parents and students about differentiation.

Staff Development at More Advanced Levels of Proficiency

Teachers who are comfortable with basic routines of differentiation and who comfortably use a number of instructional strategies to differentiate content, process, and product are ready to explore differentiation in greater depth. While guided workshops, advanced readings, and opportunities for collaboration with peers and specialists remain important to teachers at greater levels of proficiency with differentiation, another aid is to work with proficient teachers to develop differentiated curriculum that stretches their own competence while generating materials valuable to other, less proficient teachers who are learning to differentiate as well. Teachers at a more advanced level would also benefit from multipart sessions or an extended session on a single topic. Staff development at a more advanced level of proficiency might include

  • Exploring various models of differentiation.
  • Selecting key concepts, principles, and skills for a lesson or unit.
  • Designing differentiated lessons and units around key concepts, principles, and skills.
  • Application of more sophisticated instructional strategies that invite differentiation.
  • Dealing with issues of assessment and grading.
  • Effective use of alternative assessments.
  • Working collaboratively with students to build a more effective and responsive classroom.
  • Coaching and scaffolding for student success.
  • Specialized approaches for specific learning needs.
  • Means of evaluating degrees of success of differentiation in the classroom.

Extended Study

In time, some administrative leaders and teachers will become in-house experts. These educators, too, will need continued honing of their understanding and skills in order to grow. Their staff development will likely include developing differentiated curriculum and assisting in the implementation of differentiated instruction on a schoolwide or systemwide basis, as well as areas of focus proposed by group members. Staff development opportunities may include teams working over extended periods of time, attendance at national and state conferences related to differentiation, and extended course work. Working with colleagues from different schools or districts is particularly important at this level.

A Productive Focus for Leadership

Addressing the specific learning needs of teachers in a way that makes the concept of differentiation more accessible and relevant to them as individuals is perhaps the most fundamental role of leaders for differentiation at every stage of district growth. A coherent and high-quality staff development plan for supporting differentiation also provides our best platform for demonstrating the power of the differentiation concept itself. Further, such a plan continually provides information useful in effectively adapting growth plans and in assessing district or school progress toward its goals.

Resources for Staff Development on Differentiation

Association for Supervision and Curriculum Development. (1996). *Differentiating instruction for mixed-ability classes* [A Professional Inquiry Kit]. Alexandria, VA: Author.

Association for Supervision and Curriculum Development. (1997). *Differentiating instruction* [A Video Staff Development Set, with Facilitator's Guide]. Alexandria, VA: Author.

Association for Supervision and Curriculum Development. (2000). *Differentiating Instruction* [Professional Development Online course]. Alexandria, VA: Author. Available: http://www.ascd.org.

Continuation of Systemic Growth Toward Differentiation

7

C areful *initiation* of systemic growth toward more pervasive and more effective differentiated instruction is essential in charting a defensible and worthy course for change. Focused and creative *implementation* strategies translate vision into action. The third phase of change—*continuation*—is perhaps easy to overlook. Making plans and taking action seem like enough, but the work is not over yet.

Schools and districts have cultures of their own. Individuals in schools and districts have deeply rooted belief and value systems. If leaders attempt to alter only the veneer of the cultures and beliefs that define us, our early efforts are likely to fall short of sustained change.

A personal analogy familiar to all of us is New Year's resolutions. We make them. We mean to keep them. The resolutions generally would improve our lives in some way, and our intent is to change in the positive ways we fashion for ourselves at the start of a new year. In the vast majority of instances, however, the familiarity of habit combines with the pressures of daily life to obliterate our good intentions. Without the structures of the continuation phase of change, the resolutions of the initiation phase and the "January actions" of the implementation phase are likely to be buried by the inertia of winter. Change will once again have a short shelf life.

In the continuation phase of change, leaders need to establish and execute plans that address the core of who we are and what we do as a school or district. These plans must address our inclination toward inertia by modifying structures and processes that ultimately shape what we do. They must, over time, redefine our culture. "Structural change that is not supported by cultural change will eventually be overwhelmed by the culture" (Schlechty, 1997, p. 136).

Four areas are key to continuing systemic growth toward differentiation because they shape the system in ways that can, over time, shape our values. These areas are (1) hiring school personnel who either have or are open to differentiation as a teaching philosophy, (2) providing teachers with a curriculum that supports differentiation, (3) providing educators with support and accountability for their growth in differentiation, and (4) encouraging changes in classroom instruction by examining outcomes.

The Importance of the Hiring Process

Combined with thoughtful staff development and the bully pulpit to promote teaching in response to academically diverse classrooms, an effective way to support differentiated instruction in the long term is to bring on board educators new to the district who have already created, or want to create, responsive classrooms. Turnover in teaching is inevitable. Using that reality to support differentiation makes a great deal of sense in promoting long-term systemic change.

Leaders can structure the hiring process to unveil an applicant's teaching philosophy and practice. As a first step, make sure that interviewers are knowledgeable about differentiated instruction so that they are able to evaluate a candidate's training, portfolio, experience, and responses to questions. Second, include questions about academic diversity in the classroom in the interview protocol. A district can make its hiring function easier by developing some consistent questions that can be asked of all applicants who reach the interview stage. Some possible interview questions include the following:

• How do you handle academic diversity in your classroom/school?

• What kinds of strategies do you use to handle varied student approaches to learning?

• What students with special needs have you taught, and what instructional approaches did you use to help them?

• How do your instructional goals take into account the varying learning needs of individual students or groups?

• What do you do when a conflict exists between covering the material in the curriculum and gaps that you observe in student understanding?

- How do you envision your use of grouping for instruction?
- What kinds of assessment do you use and how do you use them to shape instruction?
- Where and how do you provide students with opportunities for choice?

Third, you might consider asking applicants to submit portfolios that demonstrate evidence of differentiated instruction strategies such as tiered lessons, interest centers, analysis of learning profiles, and so on.

Of course, preservice teacher preparation is a major long-term issue in securing staff with both the *skill* and *will* to create academically responsive classrooms. Although preservice teacher preparation is largely completed by the time hiring begins, schools and districts can nonetheless over time have an effect on preservice teacher preparation for differentiation.

Some districts have initiated dialogues with schools of education requesting preservice training that prepares young teachers to begin their careers with confidence in academically diverse classrooms. Others have collaborated with teacher education programs to create professional development schools in which academically responsive instruction is a shared goal between the university and school or district. Still other districts have matched student teachers with veteran teachers who actively differentiate instruction to take advantage of the power of early modeling in shaping novice teacher practice. Finally, some districts find success in pairing first-year teachers with district mentors who model and promote differentiation as a way to enculcate in new teachers a belief system that benefits academically diverse student populations. Few new teachers have had the opportunity to refine teaching competencies necessary to be highly skilled with differentiation (Tomlinson et al., 1997). But new teachers are more likely to develop those competencies if they are schooled in the need to do so and surrounded by colleagues and a culture that commend and model the expectation.

While hiring teachers who are ready for the challenge of today's varied student population is crucial, the hiring of administrators and support personnel on goals of differentiation is no less essential. Because the role of principals in school change is so profound, newly hired principals need to be strong believers in responsive instruction. They must have (or be willing to acquire quickly) the skills necessary to support differentiation, and they need to understand and accept the leadership role they are expected to fill in this regard. Unfortunately, we have seen that when unsupportive and uninformed principals replace former champions of responsive teaching, schools tend to lose ground quickly in their strides toward effective differentiation (Callahan et al., in press-b).

Similarly, for continuation of change, when guidance counselors, social workers, media specialists, and technology specialists join a school or district staff they should share the expectation that their work will include leadership to extend classrooms that meet the needs of individual students. Finally, newly hired resource specialists (special education, gifted education, second language, reading, etc.) must be willing and able to serve simultaneously as differentiation specialists and specialists in their own domain. Such a role suggests the capacity to collaborate, work effectively in regular classrooms, and be flexible in responding to the needs of a wide range of teachers and students, in addition to their own domain of expertise.

Integration of Differentiation into District Curriculum

As the process advances to provide for academic diversity in classrooms, teachers sometimes find themselves struggling against a district curriculum that seems more standardized than differentiated. This situation is aggravated if the curriculum is largely a collection of topics, facts, and skills—a difficult kind of curriculum to differentiate. To support continuation or institutionalization of differentiated instruction, the written curriculum needs to reinforce the expectation of academic responsiveness and help teachers in the difficult task of responsive teaching. A plan for creating differentiated curriculum thus becomes very important at least by the continuation phase of school or district change.

Guidelines for Creating Differentiated Curriculum

What does a curriculum that supports differentiated instruction look like? This question is relatively new for educators. Models for effectively differentiated curriculum are just now evolving. Nonetheless, knowledge of effective curriculum in a general and formative sense of what it means to teach diverse learners well can provide some guidelines for making progress in this area.

The curriculum should have a strong conceptual base. Curriculum based upon discrete and loosely connected facts and skills is difficult to differentiate—or, for that matter, teach—effectively. Conceptual learning helps all students develop frameworks of meaning, attach what they are learning to their own lives and experiences, make connections within and among disciplines, retain what they learn, and use what they learn better than does fact-based teaching (see, e.g., Caine & Caine, 1994; Erickson, 1998; National Research Council, 1999; Wiggins & McTighe, 1998). If students have only facts and skills to learn, differentiating how those are learned may be a trivial modification in the classroom and is an unlikely strategy for meeting the broad needs of learners. In addition to setting the stage for more powerful learning, concept-based curriculum has clear benefits for differentiation as well. Concept-based curriculum promotes teacher clarity about common learning goals, gives a clear and powerful focus of instruction for struggling students, provides a platform for meaningful extension of learning for advanced learners, and crosses cultures to connect with students of varied backgrounds. Concept-based curriculum is challenging to create and vastly worth the effort.

The curriculum should specify topics, facts, concepts, principles, skills, and attitudes that are to be taught and learned. Writing new curriculum with these characteristics results in complete rather than sketchy curriculum, raises the cognitive level of the curriculum, facilitates intra- and interdisciplinary connections, and sets the foundation for differentiation that offers each learner comprehensive and powerful learning experiences. (To learn more about concept-based curriculum and all its elements, see the resource section listed at the end of this chapter.)

The curriculum should demonstrate both structure and flexibility. Curriculum needs structure so that teachers know what is expected of them. Benchmarks set clear expectations about what students are expected to master. But benchmarks are goals, not limitations. Benchmarks should be like semipermeable membranes of living cells, with fluid boundaries, to provide for different levels of student readiness. Differentiated curriculum should provide suggestions about what to do if a student has already mastered the benchmarks for that grade level and about what to do for a student who does not yet have the requisite skills to tackle the prescribed material for that grade. Aligning benchmarks across grade levels and putting the benchmarks for multiple levels in each teacher's hands will help provide that support. Curriculum design is also a place to deal with teachers' feelings of ownership of topics, materials, and skills. A topic may be designated, for example, as assigned to 4th grade. Certain limited, key materials may be specified as off limits for teachers in other grades so that 4th grade teachers can make the best use of unit materials. On the other hand, skills and concepts cannot belong to a particular grade level. To grow and learn, students must be allowed to move ahead in a given skill "ahead of time," and conceptual links are desirable in a variety of grade levels. Inviting teachers to make and specify these distinctions in their written curriculum can establish parameters without school walls.

The curriculum should be carefully linked to standards, texts, and other curriculum-defining documents. While standards, textbooks, and similar documents inevitably make poor curriculum if they are all we teach, they are nonetheless important in teachers' lives. Differentiated curriculum should help teachers see how they can (1) maintain accountability for designated facts, skills, and ideas; (2) present them in a meaning-rich context rather than as a list of largely disconnected items; (3) honor student differences while dealing with the need to prepare students for a single test or benchmark assessment; and (4) be both accountable and creative in their work. If we write curriculum more slowly to accomplish those goals, so be it. High-quality written curriculum is the best hope for raising our professional sights about what our students should learn and how we should teach.

The curriculum should use differentiation strategies suited to the nature of the discipline and needs of learners at a given grade level. The relatively sequential nature of math (as it is typically taught) may lend itself to differentiation that includes both increased complexity and sequential acceleration. Social studies may be more likely to keep a consistent focus on the topics and concepts prescribed at each grade level while incorporating tiered lessons, interest-based explorations, and extended projects. A language arts curriculum might consider holding genres and styles of writing consistent across students at a grade level, but varying the level of reading material used within that genre, and increasing the level of skills and complexity in writing. Physical education may focus largely on escalation of skills from a student's beginning point. A complex science curriculum may hold content steady, but lab opportunities and student products can vary. Each discipline and grade level within a discipline has its own personality, and differentiated curriculum should be appropriate to the nature of the discipline, the particular facets of the discipline being taught, and the needs of the learners who encounter the curriculum.

Examples of differentiation in written curricula should exemplify best practice. Written curriculum can be an excellent staff development tool with the capacity to show teachers elegant uses of a wide range of instructional approaches that can meet the needs of academically diverse learners. Teachers under the press of daily demands too readily "adapt" approaches in ways that make them easier to use—while compromising the intent of the strategy. Written curriculum allows curriculum developers to stress particularly powerful strategies and to model many strategies as they would be most effectively implemented.

The curriculum should incorporate model units. Having a sequence of fully differentiated units on paper for each subject and grade level in that subject would be ideal. That approach may be feasible over time. In the early stages of writing differentiated curriculum, educators must construct the conceptual framework for each subject and grade level. The curriculum should also provide suggestions for how to differentiate. In addition, the curriculum guide should include one or more differentiated model units. There is no greater teacher than a model. Particularly for curriculum content that is required of all students at a given level, powerful staff development provides teachers with *written examples* of precisely how the curriculum framework could be both taught and differentiated in a unit format.

The model differentiated units should include actual examples of differentiated activities and products, differentiated resources, and differentiated modes of assessment. The units should model excellent concept-based teaching. Curriculum developers would make a wise investment of time in annotating the model units, explaining why they have chosen the routes they have specified so that teachers who use the units will not only see a "what" but also a "why."

Providing these fully developed units increases the likelihood that differentiated instruction will actually take place in the classroom. The differentiated units also serve to increase teacher and administrator familiarity with the concept, provide a model for teacher thinking and planning, and emphasize the district's commitment to accommodating academic diversity.

In setting out to develop differentiated curriculum as part of the school or district change initiative, one should consider the reality that most school districts have few curriculum development experts. Providing sustained and high-level guidance for curriculum writing is imperative. In some instances, expert teachers may fill that role. In other instances, curriculum specialists may provide leadership. While expert guidance from outside the district can be valuable at key points in the curriculum development process (e.g., setting a direction, developing a format, getting started, guiding curriculum alignment, and critiquing what is developed), expertise must be built in the district among personnel who are on-site over time, and who can provide sustained guidance toward creating a coherent curriculum for the school or district.

Teacher Support and Accountability

At other points in the book, we have written about the need for intelligent and consistent support for teachers as they attempt to become more responsive to the varied learners they teach. Moreover, we ought not hold teachers accountable for tasks that we have not prepared them adequately to perform and for which we have not supported them adequately throughout the learning process. Teacher support should happen throughout the initiation and implementation phases of the change process, and beyond. At the continuation stage of change, formal assessment of growth (vs. self-assessment and peer assessment only) generally needs to be addressed.

Because they are charged with formal assessment as well as support responsibilities, administrators must be equipped to play both roles meaningfully and fairly. At the minimum, an administrator should be able to recognize differentiated activities in the classroom, judge their appropriateness for a particular unit and particular learners, evaluate their instructional effectiveness, and be able to suggest alternative strategies as necessary. Administrators themselves must also be accountable for the support and guidance they provide.

In instances where administrators are assessing the presence or quality of differentiation in subjects where they lack experience and expertise, someone who is an expert in the subject can be available to provide guidelines on what to look for during observations. One such example is represented in Figure 7.1, developed by an English/Language Arts Specialist for principals and other administrators who would ultimately provide both support and assessment in English classrooms.

A number of years into its change initiative, one district asked principals to give regular written feedback to teachers about their growth in differentiating instruction following observations and in their yearly evaluations. Working in conjunction with central office staff, principals analyzed their own written comments for quality and specificity of feedback related to differentiation. Central office staff and principals were able to use the analysis process to establish goals for both the district and the principal related to support for teachers in the upcoming year.

Tools for Assessing Differentiation in the Classroom

In deciding on tools that provide high-quality feedback to teachers related to differentiated instruction, districts may prefer to use models developed by others or to develop their own tools. In either case, the tools or instruments should (1) address differentiation in the context of high-quality curriculum and instruction, and (2) be closely aligned with those areas in which the district has provided consistent and effective support. Teachers must always have a major voice in the selection and construction of feedback tools, how those tools will be applied, and how results will be used. Whatever formal assessment tools are ultimately used, they should have room to accommodate teacher variance. Remember the significance of providing differentiation for teachers, exactly as we ask them to provide it for students, based on readiness, interest, and learning profile. That teachers grow in their capacities to respond to student variance ought to be a nonnegotiable, but teachers should have real flexibility in the areas they target for their own growth, the means by which they achieve the growth, and the way they demonstrate it. One example of an expert-generated teacher assessment and feedback tool is found in *Enhancing Professional Practice: A Framework for Teaching* (Danielson, 1996). This high-quality, research-based

Figure 7.1
Differentiated English/Language Arts Classrooms: What Do They Look Like?

Just one visit to a classroom will not reveal a differentiated program, but over the course of time, repeated evidence of some of the following elements demonstrates that instruction is designed to meet the differing needs of students.

The classroom should
- Allow for flexible groups.
- Foster the students' responsibility for their own learning.
- Provide a mechanism for students to get help when the teacher is busy with other students.
- Provide ongoing learning activities that students work on when they are waiting for the teacher or for the next group activity.
- Display assignment/project schedules, scoring rubrics, general procedures.

Instruction should
- Be less teacher lecture and more investigation and group sharing.
- Be less whole group and more small group or individual.
- Be aimed at different learning styles.
- Allow for a variety of responses.
- Allow for conference time between student and teacher.

Assignments should
- Vary in content, based on student need.
- Vary in difficulty, based on student readiness.
- Allow for choice based on student interests and strengths.
- Vary in time allotted.
- Vary to reflect student goals.
- Contain directions that are clear and direct enough for student and parents to understand.

To reflect ongoing assessment and evaluation, records should
- Include a writer's notebook and portfolio for each student.
- Include interest surveys.
- Document readiness for curriculum learning expectations.
- Record individual goal setting.
- Record achievement of goals.
- Allow for scoring one assignment with different scoring rubrics and for scoring a variety of assignments on the same topic.

Tests are tailored to fit the learners by offering items at different levels of difficulty. For example, a test might have the same short-answer questions for every student, but different essay questions for different groups.

Source: Christine Kaiser, English/Language Arts Curriculum Specialist, Grosse Pointe Public School System, 1999. Reproduced by permission.

rubric for teachers is aimed at helping educators reflect on and improve practice in four domains. These domains include

• *Planning and Preparation* (demonstrating knowledge of content and pedagogy, demonstrating knowledge of students, selecting instructional goals, demonstrating knowledge of resources, designing coherent instruction, assessing student learning).

• *Classroom Environment* (creating an environment of respect and rapport, establishing a culture for learning, managing classroom procedures, managing student behavior, and organizing physical space).

• *Instruction* (communicating clearly and accurately, using questioning and discussion techniques, engaging students in learning, providing feedback to students, and demonstrating flexibility and responsiveness).

• *Professional Responsibilities* (reflecting on teaching, maintaining accurate records, communicating with families, contributing to the school and district, growing and developing professionally, and showing professionalism).

For each domain and indicator, Danielson gives descriptors of performance at levels she calls unsatisfactory, basic, proficient, and distinguished.

Three particularly attractive features of this instrument are starting points for teacher assessment. First, the tool casts differentiation where it belongs—not as a separate entity, but rather as a feature of high-quality professionalism. Throughout the document, differentiation characterizes "distinguished performance." Studying the rubrics makes clear for teachers and administrative leaders alike that we must grow into the attitudes and skills of differentiation, that growth in differentiation is a career-long process, and that schools and districts that value expertise in teachers have no choice but to promote responsive instruction through every viable means. (Figure 7.2 shows just one of many instances in the framework where responsiveness to student variance is a hallmark of high-quality teaching.) Second, the model is comprehensive, addressing all elements needed for good teaching. Third, the document is intended to help teachers engage in self-reflection and goal setting—inevitably a better way to promote change than solely with external evaluation unattached to the desires of the individual to improve.

The domains of the frameworks are now available online at the Educational Testing Service (2000) Web site (http://www.teachingandlearning.org; go to "Frameworks for Teaching"). Further, a software version of the rubrics

Figure 7.2
Domain I: Planning and Preparation

Component 1b: Demonstrating Knowledge of Students

Elements: Knowledge of characteristics (intellectual, social, and emotional) of age group • Knowledge of students' varied approaches to learning • Knowledge of students' skills and knowledge • Knowledge of students' interests and cultural heritage

Element	Level of Performance			
	Unsatisfactory	Basic	Proficient	Distinguished
Knowledge of Characteristics of Age Group	Teacher displays minimal knowledge of developmental characteristics of age group.	Teacher displays generally accurate knowledge of developmental characteristics of age group.	Teacher displays thorough understanding of typical developmental characteristics of age group as well as exceptions to general patterns.	Teacher displays knowledge of typical developmental characteristics of age group, exceptions to the patterns, and the extent to which each student follows patterns.
Knowledge of Students' Varied Approaches to Learning	Teacher is unfamiliar with the different approaches to learning that students exhibit, such as learning styles, modalities, and different "intelligences."	Teacher displays general understanding of the different approaches to learning that students exhibit.	Teacher displays solid understanding of the different approaches to learning that different students exhibit.	Teacher uses, where appropriate, knowledge of students' varied approaches to learning in instructional planning.
Knowledge of Students' Skills and Knowledge	Teacher displays little knowledge of students' skills and knowledge and does not indicate that such knowledge is valuable.	Teacher recognizes the value of understanding students' skills and knowledge but displays this knowledge for the class only as a whole.	Teacher displays knowledge of students' skills and knowledge for groups of students and recognizes the value of this knowledge.	Teacher displays knowledge of students' skills and knowledge for each student, including those with special needs.
Knowledge of Students' Interests and Cultural Heritage	Teacher displays little knowledge of students' interests or cultural heritage and does not indicate that such knowledge is valuable.	Teacher recognizes the value of understanding students' interests or cultural heritage but displays this knowledge for the class only as a whole.	Teacher displays knowledge of the interests or cultural heritage of groups of students and recognizes the value of this knowledge.	Teacher displays knowledge of the interests or cultural heritage of each student.

Source: Danielson, C. (1996). *Enhancing Professional Practice: A Framework for Teaching* (p. 67). Alexandria, VA: Association for Supervision and Curriculum Development.

allows leaders to add to, highlight, or elaborate on indicators of differentiation stated in the framework, based on the particular goals and points of progress in the school or district.

Some districts or schools may prefer to develop their own feedback and evaluation mechanisms. These mechanisms, of course, allow for close alignment with local goals and emphases. Figure 7.3 provides a sample from such a document. The figure is only one portion of a longer instrument that is designed to help teachers think about adjusting the complexity of tasks based on learner readiness (Tomlinson, 1995 a, b). That tool is designed to look like the sliding knobs on a tape deck or CD. The instrument from which the figure is taken is thus familiar to teachers in the district. The observer who uses the feedback/assessment instrument—who could be the teacher— marks a point along each continuum that is descriptive of the element in the class(es) observed. Over time, a teacher should be able to see the "button" slide from left to right, indicating growth in the dimension in question. This district-created instrument, while clearly aligned with goals of good instruction (note district examples in the box at the top of the figure), allows particular focus on elements of differentiation that the district is spotlighting through its staff development.

Examining Outcomes

Although commitment to meaningful evaluation should exist throughout the change process, and pulse-taking should be frequent, once implementation has begun, leaders for systemic change should plan for periodic formal evaluation of both the processes put in place (e.g., curriculum development, staff development, collaborative partnerships, materials acquisition, etc.) and outcomes of the differentiation change initiative.

Among many important questions leaders might ask in regard to the processes are

• To what extent do stakeholders understand and share the vision about differentiation?

• Do we have evidence that a common vocabulary related to differentiation exists in the school or district?

• Are differentiated curriculum documents available and in use?

Figure 7.3

Quality in the Classroom

Key Indicators Related to INSTRUCTION (Process)

5. Students and teacher are engaged in collaborative and reflective conversation—student with student and student with teacher.
6. Teacher exhibits flexibility to respond to "teachable moments" and to alter the lesson plan based on the responses of students.
7. Students are engaged with content and tasks that are substantive and meaningful.
8. Teacher provides opportunities for students to be problem solvers.
9. Teacher indicates to students high expectations for learning; lessons have depth and students engage in critiquing their own contributions as well as the contributions of others.

The teacher differentiates instruction by:

Degree of Differentiation

• Assessing students' readiness, interests, and learning profiles.

None	Limited	Moderate	Extensive

• Offering "respectful" assignments for all learners.

None	Limited	Moderate	Extensive

• Encouraging and supporting students in discovery learning.

None	Limited	Moderate	Extensive

• Providing a range of activities that support and extend learning.

None	Limited	Moderate	Extensive

• Offering each student an appropriate pace of study.

None	Limited	Moderate	Extensive

- Are mechanisms for teachers to acquire materials needed for differentiation adequate, and are they adequately used?
- To what degree do teachers perceive that staff development is effective?
- In what ways does staff development plan for transfer into classrooms?
- To what degree does meaningful collaboration exist between classroom teachers and specialists?
- What evidence do we have that school, teacher, and administrator goals align with the district goals of differentiation?
- What evidence exists that administrative leaders are actively supporting teachers in their growth toward differentiation?
- Is differentiation being interpreted and translated into classroom practice in ways that seem likely to benefit students?
- Is budgeting/funding adequate to support systemic change toward differentiation?
- Is the feedback and evaluation system providing teachers with useful information about their work with differentiation?

Among many important questions leaders might ask in regard to outcomes are

- Is student achievement improving as a result of our growth in differentiation?
- Are there groups of students who are showing greater or lesser benefit?
- Is there evidence of more student-centeredness in classrooms than in the past?
- Do we have evidence that curriculum and instruction in differentiated classrooms are at a higher level than in the past?
- Are students more engaged in classes that are differentiated?
- Can we see any effects of differentiation on attendance? Student behavior?
- Is there evidence of higher student self-efficacy as a result of differentiation?
- Is there more student ownership and pride in work as a result of differentiation?
- Do we have evidence of a greater sense of community in differentiated classrooms? In the school?

- Are teachers feeling greater satisfaction with their work than in the past?
- Are teachers effectively using a broader range of instructional strategies or forms of assessment?

Remember to involve all key stakeholder groups in the evaluation process. What questions do administrators have? What about teachers? Parents? Board members? Students? Community members? How can you involve those groups in providing some of the answers? How can you share findings with them in meaningful ways? What will you do to make sure that findings are turned into growth-producing actions at the district and school level?

Over time, both internal and external evaluations should prove useful. In addition, combining qualitative and quantitative data collection methods paints a more complete picture of outcomes than does either approach alone.

Like most things in life and education, worthwhile evaluation is complex. Consult with someone who is knowledgeable about educational evaluation—and differentiation—as a part of your planning.

We can confidently say three things about evaluation of outcomes. First, leaders will see things they don't like, and as a result, have a chance to adapt and strengthen plans, as well as prospects for long-term success. Second, leaders will see things they think are strong. Hard-working and dedicated educators sometimes focus on areas that are not fully successful and become discouraged. To continue a change effort, we must regularly remind ourselves of our hard-earned successes. Effective evaluations can help ensure that we celebrate what works. Third, we owe it to those whose trust we hold to keep tabs on what we do. To maintain that trust is to maintain support for continued growth.

Resources on Concept-Based Curriculum

To learn more about writing concept-based curriculum:

Association for Supervision and Curriculum Development. (1997). *Planning integrated units: A concept-based approach* [A staff development video]. Alexandria, VA: Author.

Erickson, H. (1998). *Concept-based curriculum and instruction: Teaching beyond the facts.* Thousand Oaks, CA: Corwin Press.

Communicating with Parents and the Public About Differentiation

8

E ffective communication with parents spans the initiation, implementation, and continuation phases of school change. Several issues related to the topic of parent communication are significant enough to merit particular consideration.

Parents and the public tend to feel they know the right way to "do school": generally the way they saw it done when they were there. This inclination, added to a general suspicion of schools, means that leaders need to communicate often and effectively with parents about school-related beliefs, plans, and policies—especially when they vary from parents' preconceptions about how schools "should be." Experience with and information on more contemporary approaches to automobile engineering, medicine, and even recreation make parents and the public eager consumers of "new and improved" technologies in these areas. Our responsibility is to help parents become knowledgeable about the nature and benefits of contemporary approaches to both teaching and learning.

In communicating with parents and the public about differentiated instruction, school leaders walk a tightrope—being careful not to over-promise and underdeliver on the one side while articulating a vision and setting high expectations on the other. Because the concept of accommodating diversity among students is readily understood, parents may assume the content is also simple to implement. Teachers know that assumption is far removed from reality. Effective communication makes clear that while the school or district has adopted the philosophy of accommodating academic diversity, putting it into practice remains a work in progress. In return, professionals within the district must have true commitment to their own growth in understanding of and skill in implementing the concept. In this chapter, we suggest some important qualities of communication about differentiated instruction, provide some models for communication, and discuss management of the particularly challenging topic of assessing and reporting on student progress.

Qualities of Effective Communication About Differentiation

At its core, of course, communication consists of sending and receiving messages. At the very least, leaders should have a clear message, share it thoughtfully, and listen carefully to messages parents and community members send as leaders' messages are received. Effective communication has no formula. It is unique to individuals and particular contexts. In general, however, effective communication with parents and community members about the nature and intent of differentiation likely has many of the following characteristics.

Communications Should Avoid Jargon and Focus on Effects for Students

Terms that sound "new" to parents sometimes raise warning flags in them. "Differentiation" may be one of those terms. Some districts elect simply to talk with parents about plans to focus on student achievement or to help each child develop his or her abilities most effectively. Use of the term "differentiation" is optional (although including it may be necessary if the term is used commonly with staff, so that everyone is speaking a common language). What is not optional is helping parents understand that the teachers are working hard to know and serve their children better.

Communications About Differentiation Should Be Consistent

When educators and parents need to share a vision and a vocabulary related to differentiation, the language used should carefully convey consistent meanings to everyone. If particular facets of differentiation need emphasis at certain times or in certain contexts (e.g., grade levels, schools, teams, departments), communications with parents should spotlight the emphasis in a way that links parent understanding with teacher efforts.

Communication About Differentiation Should Be Persistent

Planned communication needs to happen often. Parents are busy, and they can easily overlook or forget an occasional message. Further, education has been subjected to so many fads that if regular reminders to our commitment to a concept don't occur, people are apt to assume it has disappeared, especially if leadership has changed within the district or school. People expect a "new broom to sweep clean" and tend to think that a change in principal, superintendent, or key school board members means "out with the old and in with the new." Regular reminders that an institutional commitment has been made keep the idea in the forefront. In addition, each school district has new parents every year. In a five- to six-year period of time almost all elementary parents are new. About half of the elementary parents will be gone from the school within only three years. Middle schools (except for families with multiple children) have complete turnover in three years and high schools in four. Therefore, for long-term projects, regularly remind parents (and other stakeholders) about the need to accommodate academic diversity and our methods for doing so.

Communication About Differentiation Needs to Be Interactive

Communication regarding differentiated instruction (or any initiative) should not be a one-way street. Parents and community members (*and teachers*) must have regular input regarding the effectiveness of the implementation and the clarity of the communications. Surveys, focus groups, parent meetings, staff meetings, and leadership teams are all mechanisms for checking on the quality of the communication efforts as well as of efforts toward creating effectively differentiated classrooms.

Communication About Differentiation Needs to Take Many Different Forms

An effective communication plan uses multiple modes of communication to convey messages. Among the options are parent brochures, newspaper articles, cable television, Web sites, newsletters, parent meetings, and back-to-school nights. By sharing information in many ways, schools provide parents with more communication more often. In the Appendix, Figures A.4 and A.5 offer examples of brochures designed to help parents understand differentiation. Figure A.6 illustrates an example of a communication with parents about differentiation in a specific subject area.

Communicating to Parents About Individual Learners

Communications such as those described in the previous section and illustrated in the Appendix can help parents and the public understand a school or district approach to accommodating academic diversity. But schools, particularly those that embrace the concept of seeing each child as an individual, must also address communication to each parent or guardian about their individual student and that student's progress in school. The following are three areas in which administrative leaders and teachers might want to personalize communication about differentiation, helping parents understand what the approach means for individual students.

Identifying Differentiated Assignments

Nothing is more frustrating than seeing a teacher work hard and successfully to address a learner's individual needs and not be recognized by parents. A hallmark of an effectively differentiated classroom is management of differentiated assignments in a way that doesn't call attention to itself. Sometimes we do so well that differentiation is camouflaged from everyone, including parents. Parents, of course, see only the one assignment that comes home: the one that was assigned to their child. They have no way of knowing that a teacher gave a tiered assignment or several product options. Teachers, therefore, need to have ways of letting parents know when assignments are differentiated. Chapter 9 shares one example of how a district accomplished this important form of communication with parents.

Parent Conferences

Parent conferences are a staple of most elementary schools and are also provided in many middle and high schools. Unlike back-to-school nights, which are usually focused on orientation to classes, parent conferences offer an opportunity for most parents to receive feedback about their own child's classroom performance. Parent conferences in differentiated classrooms should offer concrete evidence of individual student goals and growth in meeting those goals. Portfolios or other longitudinal work samples, for example, provide visible evidence of a student's progress in relation to goals. In classrooms where students are encouraged to analyze and be aware of their own progress, student-led or student-involved parent conferences also help communicate to parents how the teacher is adapting to individual learner needs.

Personalized Student Growth Plans

Teachers can develop report forms that are personalized and yet manageable for teachers, that involve students in goal setting, and that report clearly to parents. These formats involve teachers thinking about three kinds of goals: common goals for the entire class, goals for a subgroup of students, and goals for an individual. Students can be involved in both the planning and reporting. Figure 8.1 offers a sample personalized growth report that could be used as part of a parent conference, as an element in a portfolio, or by itself to help parents understand how differentiation is working for their child. The report is presented in the form of a letter from the student to the parents.

Report Cards: A Key Communication with Parents

Although report cards are also a form of communication to parents about individual students, they are critically important and merit expanded discussion. The issues of grading and reporting are enormous, and a well-researched body of literature on that topic continues to grow. Indeed, the issues of reporting and grades are two of the thorniest and most difficult in the implementation of differentiation, particularly at the secondary level.

Differentiation raises questions about whether to grade students on individual growth or on a standard measure of achievement. For example, should a struggling student who made great progress in a marking period receive an A even though he or she remains behind "grade-level" expectations? What does an A mean for a highly able student who progressed little if any, but whose relative achievement level was so high that an A seemed the only grade to give? If the teacher is truly differentiating, particularly according to readiness—that is, providing varied assignments and materials geared to the student's current level of skill and understanding—how would

Figure 8.1

Sample Personalized Growth Report Form for Middle Schoolers

Dear Mom and Dad,

Welcome to parent conferencing night. My teacher and I have developed the following report so that you will know what I am working on in _____ (subject area) this term.

We have some goals for our class this term. They include the following:

Academic:

_____

_____

_____

_____

Work Ethic:

_____

_____

_____

_____

In addition, my teacher has differentiated these goals for me and a group of my learning partners in this way:

Academic:

_____

_____

_____

_____

Work Ethic:

_____

_____

_____

_____

In discussion with my teacher, I've also decided on the following personal goals:

Academic:

_____

_____

_____

_____

Work Ethic:

_____

_____

_____

_____

I would like your help in accomplishing my goals by:

_____

_____

_____

Love,
(Your son or daughter)

Source: From the Grosse Pointe, Michigan, Public School System, 1999. Reproduced by permission.

she understand and assign grades?

The subject of grading in a differentiated classroom is meat for a book in itself. In the confines of this space, we can provide some thoughts for administrative leaders and teachers to think about as they consider the issue of effective grading and reporting practices, and we can propose some modifications to typical current grading and reporting practices.

Points to Ponder Related to Grading

• **We have little evidence that grades motivate students to learn** (see, for example, Kohn, 1993). Grades demonstrate to struggling students that they have little capacity to genuinely succeed. Grades hook highly able students on the pursuit of As but seldom on the joy of learning for learning's sake.

• **We have little evidence that grades communicate in meaningful or accurate ways to parents or students.** A C for one teacher may be a mark of competence and for another an indication of near failure. Besides, a C by itself doesn't give anyone useful feedback about how to improve.

• **Students persist when they experience a balance of hard work and success that stems from the hard work.** Grading solely in competition with other students (vs. at least in part in competition with oneself) ensures that some students will work so hard with so little effort that they sooner or later give up on school. Similarly, competitive grading continually demonstrates to other students that accolades are virtually a given. Those students nearly always succeed with minimal effort, resulting in their sense that good grades are an entitlement and that success need not be preceded by hard work. Good grades following minimal effort also robs students of the coping skills of persistence and resilience and leaves them ill prepared both academically and emotionally when genuine challenge does present itself.

• **Grades are necessarily equivocal.** We already "tinker" with grade books, take into account student circumstances when we assign grades, and certainly are influenced in our grading by our attitudes about and expectations for given learners. Paul Dressel (in Kohn, 1993) comments that "a grade can be regarded only as an inadequate report of an inaccurate judgment by a biased and variable judge of the extent of which a student has attained an undefined level of mastery of an unknown proportion of an indefinite amount of material" (p. 201). Acknowledging the messiness of grades rather than clinging to a sense that they are somehow pure, objective, and totally verifiable might at least begin a new discussion about grading and reporting.

Thinking a Little Outside the Box About Grading

Numerous schools and districts have already begun a search for contemporary approaches to grading and reporting, based on our knowledge of psychology, motivation, learning, and the brain. Educators want practices that are more effective than "grading on the curve." Portfolios, narratives, and exhibitions of student performance have far greater merit to motivate students to take charge of their productivity as learners than do standard report cards. These products also have a much richer potential to communicate with parents about their children. However, the purpose of this book is not to argue that we jettison all the elements of standard grades and report cards. Rather, we must make one central statement about grading and reporting, as they are inevitably a reflection of our beliefs about differentiation. *Whatever method of grading and reporting we elect to use, we must grade at least in part on student growth.* How this principle is applied may vary at the elementary, middle, and high school levels. If student differences matter enough to attend to them in instruction, we should not disregard them at the point of grading and communicating with students and parents about student progress.

To move in the direction of taking into account personal growth as a part of our grading and reporting process, we might develop policies and procedures that distinguish between achievement and other factors, such as effort and progress (J. McTighe, personal communication, 1999). We could, for example, use recordkeeping systems and reporting mechanisms that speak to elements such as

- Achievement (noted by standardized scores).
- Progress (measured against standards or individual goals).
- Growth (in comparison with self).
- Habits and attitudes.
- Work quality (Wiggins, 1999).

Disaggregation of these key variables would lead to more credible and useful reporting, regardless of whether letters, numbers, or narratives are used in the reporting. Wiggins (1998) further advises educators to think about the following approaches for report card reform:

• **Report many more subscores of performance in summarizing performance data.** Performance data should be organized to highlight a number of key curricular goals and performance factors rather than lumping together many variables into one grade.

• **Distinguish explicitly between growth-based evaluation and achievement symbolized by letter grades and numerical scores, respectively.** Acknowledging this distinction would allow both criterion-based and norm-based reporting to parents in the same card. In other words, parents would have information about how their child progressed and grew as well as how their child did in relationship to other learners. Experience demonstrates that parents want both pieces of information.

• **Report two kinds of expectation-referenced grades.** Individual expectations are determined and reported in relation to student progress in achieving individual goals in a subject area. Grade-level expectations can be determined and reported in achieving grade-level benchmarks in a subject area.

• **Analyze students' academic achievements through three kinds of data: level of achievement, quality of work, and progress against standards.** Work quality is a way to measure the caliber of the products produced at any level. Using this approach, every learner could be helped to work toward high-quality work and production at his or her level for that level of achievement.

• **Evaluate the student's intellectual character—habits of mind and work—based on established patterns over long periods of time in performance and products.** Such evaluation would allow teacher feedback that is often sorely needed by students on issues such as independence, effective class participation, and disciplined work habits.

Certainly, once school personnel arrive at some sort of consensus about grading, they need to develop published policies that delineate both a rationale for the decision and guidelines for its implementation. Not only would such a document need to be available in accessible language for parents, but parents should, of course, be encouraged to contribute to the decisions and to assess their effects over time.

Translating Ideas into Practice

A variety of possible reporting mechanisms would reflect the factors above. (Some references on grading and reporting are provided at the end of the chapter to facilitate further exploration of possibilities.) However, even some simple changes can provide some of the information needed in a differentiated classroom.

A simple change in report cards could be a format that reports both progress and relative performance level by combining letters and numbers. For instance, the report card might carry the following keys:

A—represents excellent student growth during the marking period
B—represents good student growth during the marking period
C—represents moderate student growth during the marking period
D—represents little growth during the marking period
F—represents no observable growth during the marking period

1—indicates skills and understanding below grade-level expectations
2—indicates skills and understanding at grade level
3—indicates skills and understanding above grade level

A student would then receive a grade such as *B1* or *C3*. This grade communicates to parents student progress according to particular personal goals (that can be shared in writing and at parent conferences). In addition, it communicates a student's relative standing on agreed-upon benchmarks such as grade-level standards. Note that the letter grades represent progress or growth, not effort.

A second specific way in which schools have modified reporting systems to chart both student growth and relative standing is reflected in Figure 8.2 (pp. 114–115). This section of a report card for elementary students uses a continuum to help parents understand the current status of their own student, chart his or her growth over time, develop a sense of the specific goals on which their child is working, and have a sense of how their student is progressing relative to students of a similar grade level.

A less radical departure from the comfortable may be a good starting point, particularly at the high school level where grade and rank are still powerful. At the very least, the report card could remain very "standard," but with a shift in how the teacher thinks about grading being reflected in the grades that appear *on* the report card. That is, the teacher differentiates content, process, and product so that each student has a good chance of being appropriately challenged, working with interests, and finding effective working conditions at key times during the marking period. Expectations for a given student's work are clear, and the teacher grades students based on the expectations for a particular task and student. At the end of the marking period, the teacher gives all students the same assessment, based on course-level expectations for all students. That final test may even "count" more than other work that preceded it in determining the report card grade. Nonetheless, for at least a portion of the marking period, the student was accountable for growing at an appropriate degree toward designated goals. For at least those times in the marking period, the teacher attended to the reality that we don't all learn according to the same formula, and thus attempted to help each student move forward—with understanding and competence—from a starting point. Research and experience would indicate that maximizing the student's opportunities to make sense of ideas and skills (a) does not guarantee that all students learn all things, (b) does not result in As and Bs on all report cards, but (c) proves more motivating to students, and (d) results in greater understanding and proficiency than for-mulaic instruction. At least it's a place to begin.

Report cards carry to parents part of our message about teaching and learning. As is the case with all communication, we must communicate clearly, thoughtfully, and in ways that support maximum growth of each learner entrusted to us.

To Learn More About Grading and Report Cards

Association for Supervision and Curriculum Development. (1996). *Reporting student progress* [Video staff development set]. Alexandria, VA: Author.

Guskey, T. R. (Ed.). (1996). *Communicating student learning: 1996 Yearbook of the Association for Supervision and Curriculum Development.* Alexandria, VA: Association for Supervision and Curriculum Development.

Kagen, S. (1995, May). Group grades miss the mark. *Educational Leadership, 52* (8), 68–71.

Kohn, A. (1993). *Punished by rewards: The trouble with gold stars, incentive plans, A's, praise, and other bribes.* New York: Houghton Mifflin.

Sizer, T., & Sizer, N. (1999). Sorting. In *The students are watching: Schools and the moral contract* (pp. 58–80). Boston: Beacon Press.

Wiggins, G. (1998). *Educative assessment.* San Francisco: Jossey-Bass.

Figure 8.2
Continuum of Reading Development

Pre-emergent	Emergent	Developing	Transitional	Bridging	Expanding	Independent
• May know some letter sounds. • Relies on others to read or share books. • May make up a story from pictures after repeated listening experiences.	• Knows most letter sounds. • Uses beginning sounds with picture cues and context to decipher unfamiliar words. • Associates print and sounds with meaning. • Understands concepts of print. • Retells familiar stories in sequence.	• Uses initial and final consonants, consonant clusters, and word families to decipher unfamiliar words. • Begins to integrate meaning, language structure, and phonic cueing systems. • Relies less on memorizing a text. • Begins to develop fluency with familiar texts. • Reads new patterned stories with help. • Begins to monitor and self-correct errors that interfere with meaning. • Begins to summarize stories. • Reads own writing.	• Uses some long and short vowel sounds to decipher unfamiliar words. • May read new text word-by-word but shows evidence of phrasing. • Self-corrects errors that interfere with meaning. • Demonstrates understanding through discussing or retelling. • Recalls important details and formulates a main idea. • Independently makes connections between personal experience and story or between stories. • Compares/contrasts two stories. • Uses information to form opinions. • Recognizes different genres (poetry, fiction, information). • Able to read alone for 10 minutes or more.	• Independently uses a variety of reading strategies (meaning, language structures, and phonics). • Reads fluently with expression most of the time. • Self-corrects most errors. • Makes reasonable predictions based on prior knowledge and the text. • Independently makes judgments about characters, plot, main idea. • Retellings include some of the following: details, characters, setting, sequence of events, generalization, main idea, personal reaction, evaluation. • Begins to read chapter books. • Remembers plot of a long story read over several days. • Able to read alone for 15 minutes or more.	• Retellings include some of the following: - recognition of character development - influence of setting on plot - comparison/contrast with other books - inferences. • Able to use reference materials for reports. • Reads longer, more complex books. • Able to read alone for 20 minutes or more.	• Retellings are effective and complete. • Independently makes generalizations and inferences about patterns, characters, plot, setting, genre, style, and purpose. • Independently makes connections. • Accepts challenges as a reader. • Spends quality time reading.

Most children exit kindergarten at the Emergent Level of reading. Most exit 1st grade at the Transitional Level. Most exit 2nd grade at the Expanding Level.

Figure 8.2—*continued*
Continuum of Writing Development

Pre-emergent	Emergent	Developing	Transitional	Bridging	Expanding	Independent
• Relies on pictures to convey meaning. • Writes random, recognizable letters. • Tells about own writing.	• Expresses ideas on paper. • Uses beginning/ending consonants to represent whole words. • Copies words. • Understands concepts or print. • Reads own writing. • Begins to use spacing.	• Writes complete, understandable thoughts. • Uses some temporary and some conventional spelling. • Writes from top to bottom and left to right.	• Writes two or more sequential thoughts. • Spells many common words conventionally. • Begins to edit. • Writes pieces that others can read. • Experiments with capitals and end punctuation. • Begins to collaborate or writing projects.	• Can compose a story with a beginning, middle, and end. • Uses punctuation and capitals for "I," names, and beginnings of sentences. • Begins to evaluate writing. • Helps others edit. • Begins to revise by adding description/detail.	• Begins to develop paragraphs. • Writes with detail and organization. • Uses strategies to spell (sound patterns, graphic patterns, meaning). • Writes for various purposes. • Begins to revise by deletion. • Begins to use 5-step writing process: prewriting, organizing, writing, revising, editing.	• Begins to organize information into a report. • Uses a variety of sentence structures. • Develops editing and proofreading skills. • Employs several strategies to spell difficult words. • Uses quotation marks. • Revises by reorganizing or adding literary devices. • Uses 5-step writing process independently.

Most children exit kindergarten at the Emergent Level of writing. Most exit 1st grade at the Bridging Level. Most exit 2nd grade at the Expanding Level.

Source: From the Grosse Pointe, Michigan, Public School System, 1999. Reproduced by permission.

Growth Toward Differentiation in Context: A Case Study of Change in Process

9

To this point, this book has discussed planning elements likely to facilitate systemic growth toward differentiated or academically responsive instruction. In this chapter, we present a case study of a specific district to illustrate ways in which the various elements come together in a distinct plan to initiate, implement, and ultimately institutionalize differentiation as a way of thinking about teaching and learning.

Of course no two districts or schools are alike. Because profiles and needs differ, no two districts or schools would adopt exactly the same plan for growth toward differentiation. Our goal in this chapter, then, is not to commend a particular change plan, but rather to illustrate how one district thought about initiating and implementing a philosophy of differentiated instruction—and how that district is looking ahead to institutionalizing differentiation as a means of addressing the particular needs of its students, staff, and community. Each section of the chapter offers a description of events and actions in the district, as well as a *commentary* designed to make explicit some important principles or insights derived from what transpired in the district during an initial planning year and the first year of serious focus on differentiating instruction in mixed-ability classrooms.

Background and Rationale for Action

The Charlottesville City Schools, as the name suggests, serve the city in west central Virginia that grew up around Monticello and the University of Virginia. This system is the smaller of two districts serving the greater Charlottesville area and has become a largely bimodal district over the past few decades in that the Charlottesville City Schools serve two populations with particular learning needs. In addition to a relatively smaller "typical" student group, the district also serves a large group of students from low socioeconomic settings, many who need extra support to succeed academically. The district also serves a large population of students who, by virtually any measure, would qualify as academically gifted. The district has a long history of excellence in vigorously attending to the needs of the full academic spectrum of learners and takes great pride in its reputation for thoughtful and creative educational programs.

Until recently, programs for students identified as gifted have largely taken place in pullout programs—within schools for primary-aged learners, and at a centralized site for elementary and middle grade students. The pullout programs were highly regarded by participants and their parents, and were, in fact well conceived, well planned, and well delivered.

Two years ago, the district began to deal actively with some tensions inevitably caused by services for highly advanced learners that are predominately separate from the general classroom. In this district, the high-ability population is quite large. When some students are identified as gifted and leave the classroom for special services, a good number of students are left behind who could likely also benefit from advanced learning opportunities. A second problem was created because a relatively small number of students from low socioeconomic and minority groups were identified as eligible for advanced services, despite continuing efforts to include able students from these populations. Even those low economic and minority group students who *were* identified often disliked having to leave the classroom—and their peer groups—to take part in advanced learning opportunities. Third, in a district where both staff and constituents find the district's diversity to be highly attractive, programs that appear "separate" and "special" seem to be out of sync with the nature of the district. Finally, when the job of a specialist becomes "fixing" a school for a particular group, the job of the general classroom teacher seems to cease being able to attend to the specific learning needs of that group. This situation limits the likelihood that high-end activities routinely take place in the general classroom, which constitutes the majority of advanced learners' day, year, and school career. The School Board, district leaders, and community members struggled with these issues over time.

The superintendent of the Charlottesville City Schools therefore asked several district leaders, including the director of services for gifted learners, to investigate avenues through which the district could (1) continue its tradition of excellence in providing advanced learning opportunities and (2) eliminate many or most of the tensions caused by the current mode of serving highly able learners. This investigation started the journey toward differentiation for this district and its schools.

> **Commentary:** Districts make a move toward differentiation for a variety of reasons, sometimes more than one. In some instances, a primary motivator is making services for students with learning problems more inclusive in the general classroom. Sometimes a primary motivator is to maximize the learning focus and time for students with English as a second language. The impetus to stress differentiation occasionally is simply the recognition that the district population is becoming more and more heterogeneous. The effort can be driven by issues related to services for learners identified as gifted, as was the case in this district. Frequently, a district must attend to several of these needs simultaneously.
>
> A few key factors related to the start of the Charlottesville City Schools' movement toward differentiated instruction in general classrooms were:
>
> • The area targeted for change in this district—service delivery to high-end learners—was familiar.
> • The goal of the change was in harmony with the culture of the school district: to address effectively issues of both equity and excellence.
> • This goal had at its core a desire to make decisions that would benefit all learners in the district—not just in rhetoric, but in practice.
> • In addition to services for advanced learners, the district has numerous services for its large population of struggling learners, operating both in and out of the general classroom. A new differentiation effort would not supplant those programs and services, but rather focus on upgrading the level of thought and richness of instruction that would provide the core of the struggling learner's day in the general classroom.
> • The goal of the School Board and other leaders was not to lessen focus on the needs of high-end learners, but rather to examine alternative ways of ensuring that their needs were met at an equally high level of quality as had been the case in past years.

These factors continue to be important in the decision-making process of the district as its journey evolves toward more responsive classrooms.

Developing and Presenting a Systemic Plan

For several months, the district's director of services for gifted learners, along with other district administrators and several teaching specialists, studied a wide range of ways in which districts deliver services to advanced learners. This time of careful study included visits to sites in several locations, attendance at national conferences, and even taking part in university-level coursework.

Relatively early in the study, differentiation of instruction in the general classroom appeared to match the district's needs and goals. Finding a specific delivery system to ensure that the appealing philosophy of differentiation might take root and grow in the district's many classrooms took longer. In other words, a viable systemic plan was required.

In search of a framework to guide implementation, the study group learned about a collaboration/consultation model developed by Mary Landrum from Kent State University. This service delivery model, it seemed, offered an organized and tested way to make certain that the instructional approach of differentiation could be translated into school and classroom reality. The consensus of the study group was unanimous.

With this confidence, the study group made a formal presentation of differentiation and the collaboration/consultation model to the district superintendent. He, too, felt the combination was a good match for the district's needs. The director of programs for gifted learners then presented both the instructional approach (differentiation) and service delivery model (collaboration/consultation) to principals of the district's K–8 schools.

Eager to implement the new approach in a careful and manageable way, the superintendent asked for two schools to pilot differentiation using the collaboration/consultation approach. Because the newly proposed plan met a need recognized by principals, all seven principals ultimately volunteered.

Next, each principal discussed with his staff the newly proposed instructional approach and service delivery model. In each instance, open conversation took place about potential positives and negatives, effect on teachers and students, possible parent concerns, timetables, and so on. Each faculty group made an independent decision about whether to participate, when, and to what degree. Five of the seven schools opted for participation in the pilot year: three for full participation, and two for participation at some grade levels only. All schools planned for participation by year two.

Throughout this decision-making process, the superintendent reported to the School Board on options, decisions, and participation levels. The Board was supportive of the change as well as the approach to the change.

> **Commentary:** Several important features were a part of the district's decision-making process, as follows:
>
> • Careful study of options (including investigation of both theory and practice) ensured a knowledgeable decision.
> • School Board, central office staff, school administrators, and teachers began the journey toward differentiation together by building some common understandings and vocabulary.
> • All educators who might be affected by the change had a voice in the decisions.
> • Differences in schools were honored in the decision-making process (thus modeling differentiation for faculties).
> • The district adopted both an instructional philosophy (differentiation in mixed-ability classrooms) and an implementation framework (collaboration/consultation), thus agreeing both on where they wanted to go and how they planned to go there.

Gearing Up

During the spring and summer months before the new school year started, the district undertook several important steps toward initiation of the differentiation change. These steps intended to provide initial preparation for three groups of stakeholders: classroom teachers, specialists, and parents.

First, district personnel met with each participating faculty group to outline precisely how the new approach would work during the first year. Also, Landrum met with each faculty; she served as a consultant to the district for three years in implementing the collaboration/consultation delivery system and assisted with staff development as well. These meetings outlined roles and expectations of classroom teachers, specialists, and the district—including staff development, shared planning, and classroom implementation.

Second, district staff met with parents in each participating school. In addition to allowing district leaders to share a rationale and plans for the change, the meetings provided ample opportunity for parents to ask

- Guaranteeing time for teacher planning.
- Ensuring that the classroom teacher is not alone in responsibility for translating differentiation into the classroom.
- Ensuring the ongoing presence in each participating classroom of an expert in high-end teaching.

Beginning the Implementation Process in the Classroom

During the first year of the differentiation initiative, and with the nonnegotiables in place and functioning appropriately, classroom teachers and specialists in gifted education began the process of planning, carrying out, and assessing the quality of differentiated instruction. During this time, at least four key stages occurred.

During the first month of school, because of prior experience with developing academically responsive classrooms, the specialist planned virtually all of the differentiated lessons based on what the classroom teacher wanted to accomplish. The specialist also carried out virtually all of the differentiation during the first month. The classroom teacher, however, had specific observational responsibilities during each differentiated lesson. The classroom teacher used an observational checklist designed to help her focus on ways in which various students responded to the high-end task that the specialist was modeling. She also made recommendations, based on the checklist observation, related to who might need still-further challenge, who might need support in achieving the task at hand, and students who seemed to be functioning at a comfortable level of challenge.

As the second month came to a conclusion, the specialist and general classroom teacher began more of a shared planning and execution of differentiated lessons, but the specialist still took the lead. Often at this point, for example, the specialist would begin the differentiated lesson for the whole class, with the teacher performing a specific task part of the way through the lesson. At an appropriate point, the specialist might say to the class, for example, "Your teacher will now tell you what your job is for the rest of the segment and where you will work to complete your task." Or the specialist might say, "Now, I'm going to work with some of you on the next step, and your teacher will work with others of you on the next step."

questions. Parents of many of the high-end learners previously served in the district's pullout program were predictably skeptical. Parents received assurances that they would be continually informed about the change initiative, including receiving consistent information about what was taking place in their students' classes and having an opportunity for formal responses to the change at the end of the first year of implementation.

Third, preparation of specialists, whose role was to work collaboratively with classroom teachers, began in earnest for changes that lay ahead for them. This preparation included three components. Initially the specialists, all of whom had served high-end learners in pullout settings, visited sites in other districts where differentiation and collaboration/consultation were in use. These visits allowed the specialists to see what the approaches looked like in action, and to talk with other educators who were engaged in a similar change process. In addition, each specialist was offered the opportunity to continue in a dramatically new role as specialist or to be transferred to a general classroom setting in the district. Finally, the district began to provide staff development opportunities for specialists, including summer workshops at the district level and attendance at an intensive summer institute on differentiated instruction. Some interested classroom teachers also participated in these early staff development options.

> **Commentary:** During this portion of the initiation phase, several components seemed particularly vital to district leaders, as follows:
>
> - Groundwork was clearly laid for what was ahead for central stakeholder groups.
> - The opportunity to visit sites where the model was at work enabled specialists to understand much more clearly (to see literally) what their work would be like. The result was that all of the specialists opted to stay with the change model. Prior to visits, some had been quite skeptical. The equivalent of one full-time specialist was assigned to each participating school.
> - Site visits also allowed district leaders and specialists to analyze differences in sites where differentiation was working effectively and sites where it seemed rougher. This early discussion served as important troubleshooting for the first year of implementation in Charlottesville City Schools.

• Site visits helped district leaders and specialists understand that growth toward differentiation is evolutionary, and while they could accomplish many things the first year of implementation, they could not achieve perfection.

• Skepticism on the part of some parents was anticipated and honored. District personnel understood that (a) these parents valued quality education for their children, (b) the parents had learned over time to distrust that the general classroom would consistently provide high levels of challenge, and (c) the district would have to accept the distrust and try to establish a new level of trust of the general classroom. Unless the new approach could earn parent trust by appropriately addressing advanced learner readiness and interest, its life span would be short.

• The district sought outside professional help both in understanding differentiated instruction itself and in planning for systemic implementation.

The Nonnegotiables

As a part of the collaboration/consultation delivery model, the district and participating schools agreed to nine nonnegotiables. These imperatives are based on experience and research with differentiation, collaboration, and the change process. Because changing services for gifted learners was at the heart of the new direction in Charlottesville City, several of the nonnegotiables focus on this group. In other settings, they could as easily be written to focus on another group (such as second-language learners) or on several groups of learners. The nonnegotiables were:

• Administrative support—Without principal as well as district leadership enthusiasm and cooperation, opportunities for growth are greatly diminished.

• Volunteer participation—The district believed that differentiating for teachers and schools was as important as differentiating for students. No school or teacher was forced to participate in the move toward differentiated classrooms. Rather, voices of individual teachers and faculties as a whole were heard and honored.

• Long-term planning days—The district and schools committed to providing participating teachers and specialists a minimum of a half-day per quarter for joint planning meetings designed to take a long look at

curriculum and instruction (for example, planning units or creating a scope and sequence for a semester).

• Regular shared planning—Teachers and specialists agreed to meet frequently to do day-to-day planning for differentiated instruction. Sometimes participants met daily, sometimes two or three times a week. Teachers met as often as necessary to ensure smooth, high-quality, and consistently differentiated instruction. Meetings might be quick, but they happened.

• Frequent follow-up support for staff—The outside consultant on collaboration and consultation met with each participating faculty group and faculty member three times during the year to help keep the collaboration process on track and to help with the quality of differentiated instruction.

• Cluster-grouping learners identified as gifted in a relatively small number of classes with volunteer teachers—Ensuring that teachers had enough high-end learners in their rooms to appear worth the effort for the change proved important. This strategy also allowed each specialist to work with no more than 12 teachers, which was extremely important in enabling them to know the teachers and students, and to have time to make a real difference in those classrooms.

• Flexible pacing—Teachers agreed to teach in a way that allowed students various amounts of time to complete tasks, rather than having the more typical goal of keeping all the students together.

• Flexible grouping—Teachers agreed to try a variety of groupings within and across classrooms as a means of matching instruction to student need. This approach included use of both similar and mixed-readiness groups within the classroom, similar and mixed-interest groups in the classroom, grouping across classrooms, and sending some students out of the ... work with the specialist when both the specialist and teacher a... need to do so.

• Ensuring a high level of challenge for advanced learne... others in the classroom.

Commentary: The participants' acceptance of the ... centrally important in the following:

• Gaining explicit commitment from partici...
• Providing systemic attention and specifie...
of differentiation.

Through the year, both planning for differentiated instruction and the instruction itself became more fully shared. Nonetheless, throughout the year, the expertise of the specialist in understanding the needs of advanced learners and strategies for managing a flexible classroom remained key to planning efforts.

Throughout the year, also, learning to plan together effectively was evolutionary as well. Early on, both specialists and classroom teachers were uncomfortable with the planning process. Even with the early weeks of specialist-led differentiation, their understanding of curriculum was different. They lacked common vocabulary. They were awkward with who should take the lead in planning at a given point. The role of the outside consultant on the collaboration and consultation model was vital in helping the teachers become more comfortable and harmonious in their planning and in ensuring effective use of the four long-term planning days.

Note that instructional planning consistently had as a clear focus the state's Standards of Learning. A goal of planning was to ensure effective instruction based on the state standards, but to do so at a high level of student thought and engagement and in the context of meaningful instruction.

Also throughout the year, a range of staff development options was consistently available for all participants in the differentiation initiative. Some staff development sessions were short-term and focused on one concrete implementation strategy such as developing graduated rubrics, assessing student readiness, or compacting curriculum. Other sessions (including two classes on differentiation) lasted longer and took a broader look at practices and implications of differentiation. Further, support was again provided for teachers to attend relevant conferences, and plans were made to send a cadre of teachers to another upcoming summer institute on differentiating instruction.

> **Commentary:** During this critical time in movement toward differentiation in the general classroom, each of the four key elements or phases was vital. Of particular interest to district leadership were the need for a clear road map of what the first few weeks of school would look like in the classroom, the opportunity observations provided for the classroom teacher to see her students differently, and insights into the planning process of teachers provided by the generalist/specialist collaborations.

The transitional procedure of moving from more specialist-centered differentiated instruction to more shared differentiation was important for everyone's sense of direction and comfort. During the first year of implementation, this plan was more evolutionary than explicitly planned. For the second year of implementation, district leaders could formalize the plan and present it to teachers at the outset of the year.

During the early weeks of the transition, structured observations gave classroom teachers a chance to see their students more clearly than ever before. Many teachers had their first real opportunity to observe which lessons were working and for whom. Teachers began to see general classroom instruction from the vantage point of a highly advanced learner who knows much more than the lesson assumes. The observations also helped teachers develop comfort with matching tasks to learner readiness. Finally, they provided an opportunity for the classroom teacher to see high-end teaching in the context of familiar curriculum.

In the curriculum planning meetings, everyone grew. While exceptions exist to any patterns noted in such settings, specialists generally lacked a sense of the nature and scope of the curriculum in the general classroom and had to broaden their perspectives on content. In general, classroom teachers tended to plan activity-based curriculum and lacked a sense of a conceptual basis for instruction as well as the ability to state clearly what students should know, understand, and be able to do as the result of any segment of learning. Classroom teachers generally did not have a sense of how to "ratchet up" instruction for all learners or what academic rigor would mean for high-end learners. Both groups needed to become more skilled at developing and using rubrics to clarify instructional goals for teachers and students alike.

Year-End Review

As the first year of implementation of differentiation came to a close in the Charlottesville City Schools, a number of valuable results and insights derived from the project.

• Faculties in all seven schools opted for participation in the project during its second year. As a result, the center-based program for gifted learners closed at the end of the first year of implementation of differentiation.

• Some of the schools so valued the role of specialist that they decided to spend discretionary funds to create additional specialist positions in their schools.

• Participating principals believed strongly that the initiative was already improving instruction for all learners. These school administrators felt they could clearly observe a significantly raised level of instruction for all learners in the differentiation classrooms.

• As a direct result of observing both the complexity and productivity of the joint planning efforts with generalists and specialists, five of the participating schools adopted curriculum planning as a key schoolwide goal for year two.

• Participation in high-end activities by students from low socioeconomic and minority groups dramatically increased over past years.

• Specialists still worked with some advanced learners outside the general classroom, particularly when the classroom teacher and specialist felt those students needed a level of challenge not offered even in the differentiated lessons. Now such groupings were short-term and flexible, directly linked with classroom curriculum, and advocated by the classroom teacher.

• Many classroom teachers were making observable strides in understanding and implementing differentiation. Some teachers, though, still showed little interest in the process.

• Everyone was quite clear that achieving the level of differentiated instruction envisioned by the district would be years in the making.

Parent and Student Response at the End of Year One

As promised, focus groups were held at the end of year one to provide parents and students an opportunity to share thoughts about the first year of implementation. Of particular interest were responses from students who had previously taken part in the district's pullout program for advanced learners. Both positive and negative responses provided an opportunity for district leaders to refine planning for year two.

Most responses from high-end students and their parents were positive. They were pleased that the new approach allowed more students an opportunity to participate in advanced-level coursework and felt that the caliber of services for students identified as gifted had not been diminished. They liked the increased amount of time in the school day focused on advanced activities. They also liked the absence of the sense of "separateness" or "specialness" that participation in the pullout and center-based programs had created. Finally, they felt strongly that the quality of curriculum and instruction in the general classroom had improved.

Note that parents knew when differentiated assignments took place in the general classroom because of a coding system devised by the classroom teachers and specialists. Teachers of younger students opted to "stamp" papers on which differentiated tasks were completed, using a rubber stamp that included the school mascot with a "Q" embedded in it. The "Q" stood for Quest, the name of the program for learners identified as gifted. Teachers designed the stamps so that they predominately reflected the school mascot with the "Q" appearing only subtly in the design. Teachers of older students ran off assignments differentiated for high-end learners on blue paper. Similar methods could be used for other students where the need exists to communicate differentiation efforts to parents.

On the negative end of the ledger, students missed doing long-term projects that were a part of pullout and center-based experiences but not of the differentiated classroom. They felt specialists were sometimes not as much "fun" in the general classroom and that specialists did not make them "think as hard" in the general classroom.

As a result of student and parent suggestions, specialists and district leaders reviewed the differentiated lessons from year one. As year two approached, the specialists and district administrators projected at least two specific changes based on parent and student comments. First, they would plan for the sorts of long-term projects students missed, which would require staff development and planning support for the collaborative teams. Second, review of the year-one curriculum indicated that assignments and tasks were consistently at a very high level of thinking and were quite comparable with tasks and assignments from the center-based and pullout programs. The teachers and administrators believe the difference between what the curriculum review suggested and what parents perceived related to the degree of complex thinking skills required in the classroom. In year two, teachers would continue to plan and monitor the level of thinking required of students, but also focus on talking with students about the kinds and purposes of thinking reflected in assignments and student work.

Looking Back—and Ahead

At the end of the first year of implementation, district leaders were pleased with the observable growth in developing differentiated classrooms. They were convinced that having both a plan for differentiating instruction and a method of promoting classroom translation were necessary for their progress, as were roles of outside experts and staff development in supporting both the approach and the delivery model. Leaders were also adamant that the role of the specialist was crucial to effective instructional planning and classroom implementation; first, the specialists had extensive prior training and experience in developing high-level curriculum as well as adapting curriculum and instruction to address learner need, and second, the specialists would have time and responsibility to serve as catalysts for collaborative work with classroom teachers. Leaders also understood that both teacher and administrator expertise in differentiation was in the fledgling stages of development and that long-term commitment to the growth process was imperative.

Looking toward later implementation and institutionalization stages, district leaders are beginning to plan strong links between differentiation and appraisal of staff performance. They have drafted an instrument to assist principals in classroom observations of differentiation and plan to revise the draft in the year ahead based on their unfolding understanding of differentiation. They have no plans to do formal assessment of teacher performance related to differentiation in year two of implementation. The second year is still a time for teacher growth and for leaders to support teachers in the risks they are taking to change their practices. Plans for staff development will grow to reflect what will likely become wider diversity of teacher readiness and interest in differentiation. In time, structures such as report cards, text adoptions, and formal curriculum development will also change to support the proliferation of differentiated classrooms. Further, the district is beginning systematic study of outcomes of differentiation for all students involved in the initiative.

Looking Beyond This District

As noted previously, schools and districts begin journeys toward differentiated classrooms for a variety of reasons. The Charlottesville experience suggests the promise of an approach to differentiation that includes a serious focus on high-end learners. All classrooms should continually attempt to raise their ceilings of performance for all learners. In fact, any pervasive change effort in a district or school ought to demonstrably benefit all learners. Any classroom that takes seriously providing consistent challenge for its most able learners will find taking place a restructuring of instructional planning, approaches, and expectations that will benefit many learners.

Often in our educational past, we have minimized the needs of high-ability learners. The Charlottesville experience suggests several very different conclusions:

• For the vast majority of learners, their teachers should learn to "shoot high" in the classroom, and then adjust support systems as necessary, rather than "shooting low" or "shooting to the middle" and then trying to adjust. Educators likely underestimate the need and capacity of nearly all learners to take part in complex thought and deal with rich subject matter. Planning first with the high end in mind is probably the best insurance policy for more engaging instruction for the class as a whole.

• Specialists in gifted education have a unique contribution to make in developing concept-based, high-level, content-rich classrooms. Their job is to know how to provide such experiences, and they are typically among a very small group of teachers in a district with that expertise. Adding their expertise to that of specialists skilled in developing second languages, providing scaffolding for reading or math development, helping students with learning disabilities compensate for processing difficulties, and so on, would provide both high classroom ceilings and support systems for all students in the classrooms.

In the end, the Charlottesville experience, and other districts successful in making noteworthy growth in differentiating instruction for academically diverse populations, suggests that change is possible. The Charlottesville experience affirms, as this book suggests, that a clear need and philosophy supported by informed and careful leaders, a systemic plan, staff development that attaches to classroom practice, supportive policies, innovative and inviting thinking, and long-term commitment provide a sound road map for an interesting and promising journey.

Planning for the "What" and the "How" of Differentiation

10

L eaders for responsive, personalized, or differentiated classrooms focus much of their professional energy on two fronts: *what* it means to teach individual learners effectively, and *how* to extend the number of classrooms in which that sort of teaching becomes the norm. Now both a rarity and a profound need, effective differentiated instruction stands a chance of proliferating where determined partnerships exist between teachers and administrative leaders with a vision of more effective classrooms, a plan to realize the vision, and a dogged will to persist. Figure 10.1 (p. 134) suggests the importance of knowing and balancing the "what" and the "how" of fostering more effectively differentiated classrooms.

The "What" of Differentiation

If we could get this teaching thing right, we'd see something like the following scenario in most of our classrooms. . . .

▼   ▼   ▼

Mrs. Clark is teaching social studies. She is fascinated by the subject she teaches and gets excited about sharing the richness of history with her students. She spends many hours each year refining her sense of what really matters in her subject, why it matters, and how she can help students understand its significance in their own lives and beyond. For that reason, she has organized her curriculum by concepts or big, enduring ideas. She poses essential questions to her students with which they grapple throughout the year to better understand their world, themselves, and the subject matter. Mrs. Clark makes every effort to answer the *teacher's* essential question for herself daily, *Why should young learners care about this stuff? What can I do to make it irresistible to them?*

▲   ▲   ▲

Because Mrs. Clark knows that her students will know history better by understanding it, using it, and finding it afoot in the world, she makes sure her students are producers of knowledge, as well as consumers of it. She ensures her students are thinkers more than copy machines with legs.

Though Mrs. Clark is quite clear about her role as the chief architect of learning in her classroom, and though she has a clear design of where she and her students must journey by the end of the year, she is also aware that she teaches individuals. They come to her with virtually the full human spectrum of proficiency levels, tastes, and preferences about learning.

For Mrs. Clark, effective teaching begins at this point. Teaching, for her, is elevated to an art form when she begins to deal with the variables that surround her. *How can I,* she asks herself, *develop personal relationships with each individual learner in a way that helps me understand him or her a little better every day? How can I arrange time, materials, groupings of learners, and even my own availability so that I can build bridges between each child and the subject matter, between each child and the possibilities waiting to be developed in every human learner? How can I enlist the learner as my partner in the bridge-building?*

To that end, this teacher becomes a hunter and gatherer of information about learners, about what they know and can do, about what works best for each person to help that student grow in knowledge, skill, and the sense of self-efficacy that comes with rising to a challenge. She diagnoses, and based on the diagnosis, she prescribes. She varies the modes of teaching and learning, ways in which students make sense of ideas and apply skills, ways in which they express and extend their learning. And she continues to observe, to be a learner herself. She converses with individuals, sets goals with them, coaches them singly, in small groups, and as a whole. She celebrates their victories and helps them celebrate one another's growth as well. She builds a community that is richer for the presence of each individual. She looks for new ways to help students both struggle and succeed.

In the end, she helps students take a measure of themselves, based in part on norms, but based also on individual growth that comes through dogged

Figure 10.1

Balancing the Equation to Make Differentiation Work

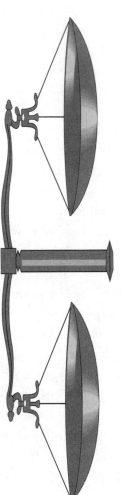
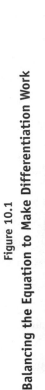

THE WHAT

● High-level, idea-based instruction using key skills to understand and apply the ideas employing key principles of differentiation:

– Flexible grouping
– Respectful activities
– Ongoing assessment and adjustment

● Modifying content, process, and product based on student readiness, interest, and learning profile using a range of student-centered, meaning-making instructional strategies

● Coaching for individual growth with the goal of moving each student as far and fast as possible

● Assessing student growth at least in significant measure according to personal growth

THE HOW

● Clarity of purpose and vision
● Systemic efforts
● Generalist/specialist partnerships for classroom application
● Time and support for collaboration
● Structured lesson (curriculum) planning and instructional evaluation
● Focused staff development with plans for transfer
● Incentives for classroom application
● Aligned and focused policies and initiatives
● Coherent leadership
● Integration with professional growth and accountability
● Formative and summative evaluation of efforts and use of findings
● Involvement of parents in understanding and contributing to assessment of change
● Persistence over time

determination and the conviction that we have power over our own destinies if we have the courage to exercise that power.

The previous statement contains the "what" of a differentiated classroom, and ought to be the standard of professionalism in the field of education. A professional is an expert in the body of knowledge that forms the core of the profession, and is also an expert in applying that knowledge, not routinely, but in accordance with the needs of each individual client (Darling-Hammond & Goodwin, 1993).

Mrs. Clark is an expert in her subject. Her expertise in that subject is not static. She challenges herself to plumb the meaning of what she teaches more deeply all the time—to understand history more fully, in her case, as an expert historian would. She is also an expert in knowing young learners. She challenges herself to extend her expertise in that sphere every day as well. The two areas of expertise come together as she joins them— connecting learner and idea in ways that dignify both. That connecting rod is artful teaching. Of necessity, such teaching is differentiated, because the learners are differentiated.

To do well what Mrs. Clark does is profoundly difficult. Attaining that level of professional commitment and competence may happen for Mrs. Clark with or without the support of wise and supportive leaders. We know from long experience, however, that Mrs. Clark will remain an "exceptional" teacher unless wise and dedicated leaders work to make her way of approaching the classroom the standard for the profession.

The "How" of Differentiation

The role of administrative leaders in fostering effectively differentiated classrooms is no less demanding, complex, or consuming than is Mrs. Clark's role in her professional environment. Such leaders are propelled by a vision of classrooms responsive to the diverse populations served in contemporary schools. They are leaders whose professional ethics drive them to reshape schools to be a better fit for a democracy that values every learner through action more than rhetoric.

School- and district-level leaders who succeed in promoting differentiation do much of their work outside the classroom, but they are not strangers to it. They visit classrooms constantly to learn from the teachers and students in them. They study effectively differentiated classrooms, and classrooms where teachers are struggling to be more responsive. In the process, leaders develop a language to talk about high-quality, responsive teaching and come to understand the difficult journey of a developing teacher who is willing to take the risk of becoming an expert teacher. Living in and appreciating the classroom as much as possible makes real both the need for differentiation and the route for achieving it.

No single leader can do what is required to refashion schools and classrooms, but what an individual leader can do is be a catalyst for teams of educators who come to share the vision and determination of the visionary. In fact, realizing a goal of more effectively differentiated classrooms calls for systemic efforts, in which leaders at the classroom, school, and district levels have key roles to play in planning, carrying out, and assessing the journey toward expert-level teaching.

Teams of leaders ensure clarity of purpose, dissemination of the vision to all stakeholders, and implementation of policies and practices that support rather than undercut the vision. Leaders for differentiation forge partnerships between classroom teachers and specialists, make time for the partners to collaborate and plan, and offer incentives for classroom implementation of the practices of differentiation. Leaders for differentiation plan and offer staff development clearly focused on personalized teaching, responsive to the developmental needs of teachers in all stages of professional growth, and designed for transfer into classrooms. Further, leaders hire with an eye on a candidate's skill and will in developing a responsive classroom, and they incorporate the necessity of growth in differentiated teaching into expectations for the professional development of every educator.

Effective leaders for differentiation lead, but they also listen. They teach and they learn. They know where they want to go, but they understand that the route will not be linear or easy. They provide steady leadership over bumps and through the dark places, and they are celebrants of growth and positive change wherever they occur. They systematically provide for short- and long-term evaluation of efforts, ensuring that what is learned from such examination is turned into positive action for additional momentum toward the goal of more effective instruction. They model differentiation. They persist.

It's Really About Commitment

We know enough about what effective teaching is to take us vigorously in that direction. We know we must teach individuals, not masses, globs, or packs. We know enough about what it takes to make change happen in schools and school districts to send us well down that road. We know change resists mandates and that it won't take place because we wish it would. Providing leadership for effectively differentiated classrooms across schools and districts is really about the will to do what we know to do. A story and a metaphor come to mind that are illustrative of what it would mean to do what we know to do in regard to investing in classrooms that meet all comers where they are and move them along as swiftly and deeply as possible.

A shipyard on the east coast of the United States was for generations run by a particular family. The family stood for high-quality ships, and they spoke their commitment to what they did by a sign that stood in front of the shipyard. It said simply, "We build good ships—at a profit, if we can—at a loss, if we must—but always good ships." The shipyard was bought by a conglomerate not too long ago. The sign came down. A question administrative leaders need to ask themselves and discuss with teachers is whether we are willing to put the sign in front of our classrooms, schools, and district offices. "We'll teach your child well—with ease when possible—with extra effort when necessary—but we will teach your child well."

William Ayers (1993), in his book *To Teach: The Journey of a Teacher*, uses a wonderful metaphor of a classroom in which bridges are built between children and learning. He makes this assertion about the role the teacher ought to play in building the bridges.

> Bridge-building requires someone to lay the first plank. Schools are often structured around the notion that the child should lay the first, the second, and virtually every plank after that. This is defeating for many youngsters. It seems clear enough to me that the teacher must be the architect and the contractor who builds the bridge. She must know the child in order to know where to put the first plank. She must also know the world, have a broad sense of where the bridge is headed, and have confidence that she and the students together can get there. And she must stay in touch with the child as the bridge takes shape. . . . (p. 77)

The bridge metaphor represents the "what" of differentiation. As a rule, we teachers throw out the planks and a few nails and wait for students to build the bridges in the same way, with the same tools. That approach is not effective in today's schools (if it ever was), and not ethically defensible. We desperately need to develop teachers who are the architects and contractors determined to help each individual learner build a bridge to success.

On the other hand, the metaphor could be rewritten to address the role of the administrative leader as well. Often leaders assume that the teacher should lay the first, second, and virtually every other plank of the bridge toward more effective classrooms. As leaders, we throw out a few planks and nails (or maybe not), and wait for the teacher to build the bridge to change. In the meantime, we may even erect obstacles to constructing the bridge. And we become grumpy because nothing gets better.

No doubt Ayers would remind leaders that they must be the architects and contractors building bridges for change—knowing the teacher as an individual, staying in touch with the teacher over time so that the bridge is built correctly to encourage the teacher to span the unknown, having a sense of the larger world of the classroom and where the bridge is headed, and maintaining the confidence that together, teachers and administrators can get where students need them to go.

There's a role for everyone. Happy building!

Appendix

▼

T
he appendix contains six documents that may be useful to school
leaders as they plan for and support growth toward more academically
responsive classrooms. Feel free to use, borrow from, or adapt the
documents.

Figure A.1 can be used to help teachers reflect on their current knowledge and personal learning goals at the beginning of staff development sessions (columns 1 and 2) and to record new insights resulting from staff
development sessions (column 3).

Figure A.2 is designed to help teachers reflect on their planning for differentiated curriculum and instruction. It is not the intent that any teacher
would target or accomplish all items on the list at any given time. Instead,
the list presents a broad range of indicators of effective planning for differentiation—all of which can guide a teacher in making decisions relevant to
given lessons or units.

Figure A.3 is similar to A.2 but with a slightly different intent. This form,
or a variation of it, can guide a colleague's observation of a teacher's differentiated class and aid the colleague in providing helpful feedback to the
teacher observed. Similarly, a teacher might use the form to reflect on his
own teaching following a lesson, lesson sequence, or unit.

Figures A.4 and A.5 provide formats useful for schools or districts when
communicating with parents about differentiated instruction—both what
the term means in general and how it might look to a parent as it is enacted
in school and district classrooms.

Figure A.6 is a sample communication regarding differentiation designed
for parents, not by a school or district, but by individual teachers. Grade
level teams, middle school teams, high school departments, or other groups

of teachers might also combine their ideas and efforts to develop this sort of communication format.

We hope you will find the documents in the appendix useful as you develop and carry out plans to make classrooms more responsive and productive for the full range of students in them.

Figure A.1

Individual Differentiation Diagnostic (KWL)			
Component:	What I *Know*/ Can Do	What I *Want* to Know/ Learn to Do	What I *Learned*
The rationale for differentiating instruction			
Evidence that supports differentiated instruction			
Setting up student expectations for a differentiated classroom			
Diagnosing student needs and assessing progress			
Using groups in the classroom			
How to manage a differentiated classroom			
Specific instructional strategies useful in differentiating instruction			
Various models of differentiated lessons			
How to select key concepts, principles, and skills for a lesson or unit			
How to differentiate content			
How to differentiate activities			
How to differentiate products			
How to talk with parents and students about differentiation			
What to do about assessment and grading in a differentiated classroom			
How to build a differentiated curriculum			
Other			

Source: From the Grosse Pointe, Michigan, Public School System, 1999. Reproduced by permission.

Figure A.2
Guides for Planning Differentiated Instruction

(Use portions applicable to your teaching/learning needs)

1. Are *you* clear on what you want the student to
- Know (facts, information)?
- Understand (principles, generalizations, ideas)?
- Be able to do as a result of this/these learning experience(s)?

2. In deciding on content, have you thought about and selected
- Alternate sources/resources?
- Varied support systems (reading buddies, tape recordings, digests, direct instruction groups, organizers, extenders)?
- Varied pacing plans?

3. Have you made plans to pre-assess student readiness so you can prepare appropriate content and/or activity? (Does the pre-assessment give a picture of understanding and skills vs. facts only? Does the pre-assessment focus squarely on items in No. 1 above?)

4. As you assign students to groups or tasks, have you made certain
- Student assignments to groups vary from previous recent ones?
- Students are encouraged to "work up"?
- Provisions are made (if appropriate) for students who need or prefer to work alone?
- Group-size matches student need?

5. As you created differentiated activities, have you made certain
- All of them call for high-level thinking?
- All of them appear about equally interesting to your learners?
- If readiness based, they vary along the continuum of the equalizer?
- If interest based, students have choices to make about how to apply skills and understandings or how to express them?
- There are opportunities for varied modes of learning to accommodate varied learning profiles?
- Each activity is squarely focused on one (or a very few) key concepts and generalizations?

Figure A.2—*continued*
Guides for Planning Differentiated Instruction

- Student choice is provided within teacher-generated parameters needed for focus and growth?
- Appropriate skills have been integrated into the activity requirements?
- Expectations for high-quality task completion are clearly delineated for students?
- You have a plan for gathering ongoing assessment data from the activity?
- You have a plan/mechanism for bringing closure and clarity to the tasks?

6. When creating assignments for differentiated products, have you made certain

- They vary along the continuum of the equalizer based on student readiness?
- They require all students to use the key concepts, generalizations, ideas, and skills to solve problems, extend understandings, and create meaningful products?
- They provide student choice options within parameters necessary to demonstrate essential understandings and skills?
- They include a core of clearly delineated and appropriately challenging expectations for the *content of the product* (what understandings and skills it must demonstrate, what sorts of resources must be used, etc.), *processes involved in production* (planning, goal-setting, time-line use, use of a process log, self-evaluation, drafts/stages, etc.), and *production requirements for the product* (e.g., what will constitute an effective video, speech, proposal, or photo essay, etc.)?
- They provide for additional criteria for success to be added by the student, and by the teacher for individual students?
- There are plans for formative evaluation and modification of the product?
- There are plans for summative evaluation by teacher, student, peers, and others (e.g., parents, "real audience") based on the product criteria?
- You have involved and informed parents as appropriate?

7. Have you also thought about

- Use of instructional strategies such as contracts, centers, interest groups, compacting, etc., that might help you vary learning options?
- Use of small groups for direct instruction (reteaching, extension)?
- Sampling students to assess understanding, group processes, and production needs?
- Meaningful tasks for reinforcement, extension, and exploration when students complete required work?

Figure A.3
Teacher/Peer Reflection on Differentiation

The following scale may be useful
(1) little or no evidence
(2) to some degree
(3) demonstrates competence
(4) demonstrates proficiency
(5) demonstrates exemplary performance

GENERAL

Pre-assesses students to determine level of understanding.	1	2	3	4	5
Assesses student interests.	1	2	3	4	5
Identifies students' learning profiles.	1	2	3	4	5
Develops a student-centered classroom.	1	2	3	4	5
Ensures respectful assignments for all learners.	1	2	3	4	5
Consistently uses flexible grouping.	1	2	3	4	5
Varies the pace of learning for varying learner needs.	1	2	3	4	5
Utilizes active learning.	1	2	3	4	5
Demonstrates escalating expectations.	1	2	3	4	5
Students' grades reflect individual growth and progress.	1	2	3	4	5

CONTENT

Differentiates using major concepts and generalizations.	1	2	3	4	5
Uses a variety of materials other than the standard text.	1	2	3	4	5
Various support mechanisms (e.g., reading buddies, organizers, study guides).	1	2	3	4	5

PROCESS

Activities necessitate that students *do* something with their knowledge (apply and extend major concepts and generalizations as opposed to just repeating it back).	1	2	3	4	5
Uses higher-level tasks for all learners (e.g., application, elaboration, providing evidence, synthesis) to provide appropriate challenge.	1	2	3	4	5

Figure A.3—*continued*
Teacher/Peer Reflection on Differentiation

Uses tiered activities.	1	2	3	4	5
Activities involve all learners in both critical and creative thinking.	1	2	3	4	5
Varies tasks along continuum of the equalizer.	1	2	3	4	5
Varies tasks by students interests.	1	2	3	4	5
Varies tasks by learner profile.	1	2	3	4	5

PRODUCT

Provides opportunities for student products to be based upon the solving of real and relevant problems.	1	2	3	4	5
Allows for a wide range of product alternatives (e.g., oral, visual, kinesthetic, musical, spatial, creative, practical).	1	2	3	4	5
Product assignments differ based on individual (or group) readiness, learning needs, and interest.	1	2	3	4	5
Teacher supports students in using a wide range of varied resources.	1	2	3	4	5
Product assignment necessitates that students conduct research.	1	2	3	4	5
Product assignment balances structure and choice.	1	2	3	4	5
Encourages students to use different avenues of exploration and a variety of media.	1	2	3	4	5
Works with individual students (or groups) to determine what form the product will take.	1	2	3	4	5
Necessitates that students apply key understandings and skills of the subject to their own interest areas.	1	2	3	4	5
Works with individual students to apply key understandings and skills of the discipline by which the product will be judged.	1	2	3	4	5
Uses both formative and summative evaluation.	1	2	3	4	5

Figure A.3—*continued*
Teacher/Peer Reflection on Differentiation

INSTRUCTIONAL/MANAGEMENT STRATEGIES

Uses compacting.	1	2	3	4	5
Uses student learning contracts.	1	2	3	4	5
Uses independent study.	1	2	3	4	5
Uses interest centers/groups.	1	2	3	4	5
Uses learning centers/groups.	1	2	3	4	5
Uses various instructional strategies to differentiate (e.g. organizers, cubing, etc.).	1	2	3	4	5
Uses high-level cooperative strategies (e.g., complex instruction, group investigation).	1	2	3	4	5
Other _____	1	2	3	4	5
Other _____	1	2	3	4	5

Figure A.4

Differentiated Programming: What It Is and What It Isn't

> The fact that students differ may be inconvenient, but it is inescapable. Adapting to that diversity is the inevitable price of productivity, high standards, and fairness to kids.
> —Theodore Sizer

Differentiated programming and instruction are big terms for what is really a simple concept—providing instruction that meets the differing needs of all students. Although the concept is simple, making it a reality in the classroom is complex. For the gifted student, it means the opportunity to advance as far as possible. For the struggling learner, it means offering support. Other students have varying abilities, learning styles, interests, and needs, all of which must be met. That is what differentiated programming attempts to do.

Differentiated Programming Is—

• Having high expectations for all students.

• Providing multiple assignments within each unit, tailored for students with differing levels of achievement.

• Allowing students to choose, with the teacher's guidance, ways to learn and how to demonstrate what they have learned.

• Permitting students to demonstrate mastery of material they already know and to progress at their own pace through new material.

• Structuring class assignments so they require high levels of critical thinking but permit a range of responses.

• Assigning activities geared to different learning styles, interests, and levels of thinking and achievement.

• Providing students with choices about what and how they learn.

• Flexible. Teachers move students in and out of groups based upon students' instructional needs.

Differentiated Programming Is Not—

• Individualization. It isn't a different lesson plan for each student each day.

• Giving all students the same work most of the time.

• Students spending significant amounts of time teaching material they have mastered to others who have not mastered it.

• Assigning more work at the same level to high-achieving students.

• All the time. Often it is preferable for students to work as a whole class.

• Grouping students into cooperative learning groups that do not provide for individual accountability or do not focus on work that is new to all students.

• Using only the differences in student responses to the same class assignment to provide differentiation.

• Limited to acceleration. Teachers are encouraged to use a variety of strategies.

Source: This document was originally developed by Susan Allan but has appeared in various forms referring to gifted and differentiated education in the Falls Church, Va.; Dearborn, Mich.; and Grosse Pointe, Mich., public schools.

Figure A.5
Q & A for Parents About Using Differentiation
to Accommodate Academic Diversity in the Classroom

Q: What does it mean to differentiate instruction?

A: Students come to school with varying levels of readiness to learn, different ways in which they learn best, and a wide range of interests. Differentiating instruction means that a teacher recognizes those academic differences and modifies classroom instruction in order to help each child reach his or her academic potential. All students are challenged without excessive stress and each student is helped to grow academically.

Q: How do teachers decide how and when to differentiate instruction for my child?

A: Standardized tests, unit tests, and quizzes are necessary and helpful for placement purposes, but do not provide enough information for teachers to evaluate students' depth of understanding. In order to evaluate depth, teachers observe throughout the year how students solve problems, evaluate students' writing, and listen carefully to the students' discussions and explanations about their thinking. Teachers use flexible grouping in order to allow students to work with the appropriate learning partners in a variety of areas.

Q: What evidence of differentiation can I expect to see?

A: Sometimes the use of differentiation is subtle. Parents may see student work come home and have no way of knowing how a teacher matched a particular assignment with their child's needs. Probably the best way of knowing how differentiation is used in the classroom is to ask the teacher. She will be able to point out particular assignments that your student worked on and tell you how the match was made between your child and the learning activity.

Q: How will I know if it is working for my child?

A: Because each student is an individual no measures of progress are absolute. Standardized learning assessments are only one measure of whether your child is making good progress. A student portfolio is an excellent way to gauge the progress a student has made during the year. Fundamentally, if the child is learning, feeling challenged but not seriously stressed, and is usually happy about going to school, you have a success!

Figure A.5—*continued*

Q & A for Parents About Using Differentiation
to Accommodate Academic Diversity in the Classroom

Q: What is expected from my child's elementary teacher?

A: The teacher is expected to know your child and to use that knowledge to match the child and the learning experience within the district's curriculum. The teacher is not expected to develop an individualized program for each student or an entirely different curriculum. Teacher expertise in accommodating academic diversity varies. The teacher is not expected to be an instant expert in differentiated instruction but is expected to grow professionally and to reach out for help from district resources when needed.

Q: What is my role as a parent?

A: Parents are a great source of information about their children. For a teacher to know as much about an individual child as the adult(s) who live with and raise that child is almost impossible. However, most parents aren't professional educators. Even for those who are, assessing one's own child's ability relative to all the others in the classroom is difficult. Most parents have not developed an in-depth understanding of the curriculum. Nor is that necessary. A parent should be involved and interested, ask pertinent questions, and follow their child's progress. A parent should not try to redesign the curriculum, but should look for structured opportunities to be involved in its development. (Many districts involve parents on curriculum committees.) Perhaps the most critical factor in being an effective parent with the schools is, while demonstrating interest in your child's education, to also respect the needs of other students and parents to claim a portion of the teacher's time and attention.

Source: From the Grosse Pointe, Michigan, Public School System, 1999. Reproduced by permission.

Figure A.6

What Does Differentiation in Math Look Like in Your Child's Classroom?

Differentiation in math is taking place in a classroom if the instruction is helping each student meet his or her potential. Does this mean that each and every student receives individual instruction in math? No, it means that throughout the year assessment and instruction are taking place in order to assure that, overall, each student is being challenged at an appropriate level. Discovering and building on students' strengths helps students achieve. For example, a student may be very strong in a topic such as geometry, but not as strong in a topic such as fractions or decimals. Using geometric shapes in the instruction may help the student understand fractions and decimals.

In today's classrooms, tests and quizzes are not the only assessments teachers use to evaluate students' progress. They also observe them when they are working independently or in small groups. Teachers evaluate students' mathematical writing that may include explanations, drawings, or diagrams. They listen to their discussions and explanations about their mathematical thinking.

Teachers need to monitor both computation (arithmetic) and conceptual understanding in the classroom. Some students may be very accurate in computation, but have difficulty applying concepts to new situations or story problems. Others may indicate that they have a high level of understanding of math concepts, but have difficulty memorizing facts or learning computation strategies. Both COMPUTATION and CONCEPTUAL UNDERSTANDING are important skills for a student's success in mathematics.

Differentiation in the area of math may look different from classroom to classroom across an entire school district:

- In some classrooms, teachers may pretest students and place them at the appropriate level of instruction for a particular unit.
- Sometimes, teachers present a lesson to the whole class and assign a variety of problems with different levels of challenge related to the lesson. Often, a math concept is new for the entire class. Teachers then need to instruct the entire class and check for mastery until it is apparent which students need more challenging problems or which students need more help to gain understanding.
- Teachers provide a variety of strategies to help students learn. They may use hands-on materials, supplementary worksheets, computer programs, or textbooks.
- At times, students may work in small groups that are randomly selected by the teacher. At other times they may work with others who are at a similar achievement level on a particular topic.
- The textbook is only one part of the students' instruction. Many math concepts can be taught with activities, worksheets, and other resources.

Figure A.6—*continued*

What Does Differentiation in Math Look Like in Your Child's Classroom?

- Students may be allowed to select computation games, strategy games, computer programs, enrichment activities, or problem-solving activities as part of their instruction.

- Teachers take into consideration that all students develop at different rates. Very able math students may have difficulty with some concepts (such as telling time or counting money) until they are developmentally ready to learn them. Trying to help a student master a topic he or she is not developmentally ready to learn can be frustrating for the teacher and discouraging for the student. Recognizing a student's readiness to learn is an important part of the teacher's ongoing evaluation.

In today's classrooms, the key to effective teaching of mathematics is to help children learn to think, reason, and solve problems. If students can be successful in a math class by simply showing what they were taught by rote without demonstrating a clear understanding of what they are studying, then the math instruction is not good enough.

In the past, simply advancing in computation was good enough. In the world today, colleges and employers are looking for thinking, reasoning, and problem-solving skills, not just arithmetic skills. Assessing students throughout the year using a variety of methods and adjusting instruction accordingly can help each student reach his or her potential in mathematics.

Source: Reprinted with permission of Mary MacDonald Barrett and The Grosse Pointe Public School System, Grosse Pointe, Michigan.

References

Amabile, T. (1983). *The social psychology of creativity*. New York: Springer-Verlag.

Anderson, R., & Pavan, B. (1993). *Nongradedness: Helping it to happen*. Lancaster, PA: Technomic Publishing Company.

Archambault, F., Westberg, K., Brown, S., Hallmark, B., Emmons, C., & Zhang, W. (1993). *Regular Classroom Practices with Gifted Students: Results of a National Survey of Classroom Teachers*. Storrs, CT: The National Research Center on the Gifted and Talented, University of Connecticut.

Archambault, F., Westberg, K., Brown, S., Hallmark, B., Zhang, W., & Emmons, C. (1993). Classroom practices used with gifted third and fourth grade students. *Journal for the Education of the Gifted, 16*, 103–119.

Ayers, W. (1993). *To teach: The journey of a teacher*. New York: Teachers College Press.

Banks, J. (1993). *Multicultural education: Issues and perspectives* (2nd ed.). Boston: Allyn and Bacon.

Banks, J. (1994). *Multiethnic education: Theory and practice* (3rd ed.). Boston: Allyn and Bacon.

Bateman, B. (1993). Learning disabilities: The changing landscape. *Journal of Learning Disabilities, 25*(1), 29–63.

Berliner, D. (1984). Research and teacher effectiveness. In *Making our schools more effective: Proceedings of three state conferences*. San Francisco: Far West Laboratory.

Berliner, D. (1988). *The development of expertise in pedagogy*. New Orleans: American Association of Colleges for Teacher Education.

Bingham, A. (1995). *Exploring the multiage classroom*. York, ME: Stenhouse Publishers.

Brandt, R. (1998). *Powerful learning*. Alexandria, VA: Association for Supervision and Curriculum Development.

Brooks, J., & Brooks, M. (1993). *In search of understanding: The case for constructivist classrooms*. Alexandria, VA: Association for Supervision and Curriculum Development.

Bruner, J. (1961). The act of discovery. *Harvard Educational Review, 31*, 21–32.

Byrnes, J. (1996). *Cognitive development and learning in instructional contexts*. Boston: Allyn and Bacon.

Caine, R., & Caine, G. (1994). *Making connections: Teaching and the human brain*. Menlo Park, CA: Addison Wesley.

Callahan, C., Tomlinson, C., & Moon, T. (in press-a). *The feasibility of high-end instruction in the academically diverse middle school. A technical report.* Charlottesville: University of Virginia, National Research Center on the Gifted and Talented.

Callahan, C., Tomlinson, C., Moon, T., Brighton, C., Hertberg, H., Imbeau, M., & Robinson, A. (in press-b). *The feasibility of high-end teaching in academically diverse middle schools: A technical report.* Charlottesville: University of Virginia, National Research Center on the Gifted and Talented.

Campbell, L., & Campbell, B. (1999). *Multiple intelligences and student achievement: Success stories from six schools.* Alexandria, VA: Association for Supervision and Curriculum Development.

Collins, M., & Amabile, T. (1999). Motivation and creativity. In R. J. Sternberg (Ed.). *Handbook of creativity* (pp. 297–312). New York: Cambridge University Press.

Csikszentmihalyi, M. (1990). *Flow: The psychology of optimal experience.* New York: Harper & Row.

Csikszentmihalyi, M., & Csikszentmihalyi, I. (Eds.). (1988). *Optimal experience: Psychological studies of flow in consciousness.* New York: Cambridge University Press.

Csikszentmihalyi, M., Rathunde, K., & Whalen, S. (1993). *Talented teenagers: The roots of success and failure.* New York: Cambridge University Press.

Danielson, C. (1996). *Enhancing professional practice: A framework for teaching.* Alexandria, VA: Association for Supervision and Curriculum Development.

Darling-Hammond, L. (1997). *Doing what matters most: Investing in quality teaching.* New York: National Commission on Teaching and America's Future.

Darling-Hammond, L., & Goodwin, L. (1993). Progress toward professionalism in teaching. In G. Cawelti (Ed.), *Challenges and achievements of American education* (1993 ASCD Yearbook, pp. 19–52). Alexandria, VA: Association for Supervision and Curriculum Development.

Delpit, L. (1995). *Other people's children: Cultural conflict in the classroom.* New York: The New Press.

Dunn, R. (1996). *How to implement and supervise a learning style program.* Alexandria, VA: Association for Supervision and Curriculum Development.

Dunn, R., & Griggs, S. (1995). *Multiculturalism and learning style: Teaching and counseling adolescents.* Westport, CT: Praeger.

Educational Testing Service. (2000). *Pathwise: A framework for teaching.* (Online). Available: http://www.teachingandlearning.org/profdvlp/pathwise/framewrk/index.html

Erickson, H. (1998). *Concept-based curriculum and instruction: Teaching beyond the facts.* Thousand Oaks, CA: Corwin Press.

Ferguson, R. (1991). Paying for public education: New evidence on how and why money matters. *Harvard Journal of Legislation, 28,* 465–498.

Fisher, C., Berliner, D., Filby, N., Marliave, R., Cahen, L., & Dishaw, M. (1980). Teaching behaviors, academic learning time, and student achievement: An overview. In C. Denham & A. Lieberman (Eds.), *Time to learn* (pp. 7–32). Washington, DC: National Institutes of Education.

Fullan, M. (1991). *The new meaning of educational change* (2nd ed.). New York: Teachers College Press.

Fullan, M. (1999). *Change forces: The sequel.* London: The Falmer Press.

Garcia, R. (1998). *Teaching for diversity.* Bloomington, IN: Phi Delta Kappa.

Gardner, H. (1983). *Frames of mind: The theory of multiple intelligences.* New York: BasicBooks.

Gayfer, M. (1991). *The multi-grade classroom: Myth and reality, A Canadian study.* Toronto: Canadian Education Association.

Gilligan, C. (1982). *In a different voice: Psychological theory and women's development.* Cambridge, MA: Harvard University Press.

Grigorenko, E., & Sternberg, R. (1997). Styles of thinking, abilities, and academic performance. *Exceptional Children, 63,* 295–312.

Hebert, T. (1993). Reflections at graduations: The long-term impact of elementary school experiences in creative productivity. *Roeper Review, 16*(1), 22–28.

Hennessey, B., & Zbikowski, S. (1993). Immunizing children against the negative effects of reward: A further examination of intrinsic motivation training techniques. *Creativity Research Journal, 6,* 297–308.

Howard, P. (1994). *An owner's manual for the brain.* Austin, TX: Leornian Press.

Hunt, D. (1971). *Matching models in education.* (Monograph No. 10). Ontario, Canada: Institute for Studies in Education.

International Institute for Advocacy for School Children. (1993). Heterogeneous grouping as discriminatory practice. *Effective School Practice, 12*(1), 61–62.

Jensen, A. (1998). The g factor and the design of education. In R. S. Sternberg & W. M. Williams (Eds.), *Intelligence, instruction, and assessment: Theory into practice* (pp. 111–132). Mahwah, NJ: Lawrence Erlbaum.

Jensen, E. (1998). *Teaching with the brain in mind.* Alexandria, VA: Association for Supervision and Curriculum Development.

Kohn, A. (1993). *Punished by rewards: The trouble with gold stars, incentive plans, A's, praise and other bribes.* New York: Houghton Mifflin.

Lasley, T., & Matczynski, T. (1997). *Strategies for teaching a diverse society.* Belmont, CA: Wadsworth Publishing Company.

Maehr, M., & Midgley, C. (1996). *Transforming school cultures.* Boulder, CO: Westview Press.

McGreal, T. (1985, November). *Characteristics of effective teaching.* Paper presented at the First Annual Intensive Training Symposium, Clearwater, Florida.

McIntosh, R., Vaughn, S., Schumm, J., Haager, D., & Lee, O. (1993). Observations of children with learning disabilities in general education classrooms. *Exceptional Children, 60,* 249–261.

Miller, B. (1990). A review of the quantitative research on multigrade instruction. *Research in Rural Education, 1*(1), 1–8.

Moon, T., Tomlinson, C. A., & Callahan, C. (1995). *Academic diversity in the middle school: Results of a national survey of middle school administrators and teachers.* (Research Monograph 95124). Charlottesville: University of Virginia, National Research Center on the Gifted and Talented.

National Foundation for the Improvement of Education. (1996). *Teachers take charge of their learning: Transforming professional development for student success.* Washington, DC: Author.

National Research Council. (1999). *How people learn: Brain, mind, experience, and school.* Washington, DC: National Academy Press.

Ohanian, S. (1999). *One size fits few: The folly of educational standards.* Portsmouth, NH: Heinemann.

Renninger, K. (1990). Children's play interests, representations, and activity. In R. Fivush & J. Hudson (Eds.), *Knowing and remembering in young children* (pp. 127–165). (Emory Cognition Series, Vol. 3). Cambridge, NY: Cambridge University Press.

Sarason, S. (1990). *The predictable failure of educational reform.* San Francisco: Jossey-Bass.

Schlechty, P. (1997). *Inventing better schools: An action plan for educational reform.* San Francisco: Jossey-Bass.

Shulman, L. (1987). Knowledge and teaching: Foundation of the new reform. *Harvard Educational Review, 57*(1), 1–22.

Sternberg, R. (1985). *Beyond IQ: A triarchic theory of human intelligence.* Cambridge, NY: Cambridge University Press.

Sternberg, R. (1997). What does it mean to be smart? *Educational Leadership. 55*(7), 20–24.

Sternberg, R., & Grigorenko, E. (1997). Are cognitive styles still in style? *American Psychologist, 52,* 700–712.

Sternberg, R., Torff, B., & Grigorenko, E. (1998). Teaching triarchically improves student achievement. *Journal of Educational Psychology, 90,* 374–384.

Sullivan, M. (1993). *A meta-analysis of experimental research studies based on the Dunn & Dunn learning styles model and its relationship to academic achievement and performance.* Doctoral dissertation, St. John's University, Jamaica, New York.

Tannen, D. (1990). *You just don't understand: Women and men in conversation.* New York: Ballentine.

Tomlinson, C. (1995a). Deciding to differentiate instruction in middle school: One school's journey. *Gifted Child Quarterly, 39,* 77–87.

Tomlinson, C. (1995b). *How to differentiate instruction in mixed-ability classrooms.* Alexandria, VA: Association for Supervision and Curriculum Development.

Tomlinson, C., Callahan, C., & Lelli, K. (1997). Challenging expectations: Case studies of high-potential, culturally diverse young children. *Gifted Child Quarterly, 41*(2), 5–17.

Tomlinson, C. A., Callahan, C., Moon, T., Tomchin, E., Landrum, M., Imbeau, M., Hunsaker, S., & Eiss, N. (1995). *Preservice teacher preparation in meeting the needs of gifted and other academically diverse students.* Charlottesville: University of Virginia, The National Research Center on the Gifted and Talented.

Tomlinson, C., Callahan, C., Tomchin, E., Eiss, N., Imbeau, M., & Landrum, M. (1997). Becoming architects of communities of learning: Addressing academic diversity in contemporary classrooms. *Exceptional Children, 63,* 269–282.

Tomlinson, C., Moon, T., & Callahan, C. (1998). How well are we addressing academic diversity in the middle school? *Middle School Journal, 29*(3), 3–11.

Torrance, E. (1995). Insights about creativity: Questioned, rejected, ridiculed, ignored. *Educational Psychology Review, 7,* 313–322.

Vygotsky, L. (1962). *Thought and language.* Cambridge, MA: MIT Press.

Vygotsky, L. (1978). *Mind in society.* Cambridge, MA: Harvard University Press.

Westberg, K., Archambault, F., Dobyns, S., & Salvin, T. (1993). The classroom practices observational study. *Journal for the Education of the Gifted, 16*, 120–146.

Wiggins, G. (1998). *Educative assessment.* San Francisco: Jossey-Bass.

Wiggins, G. (1999, October 28–29). *Making the grade.* (Handouts). Presentation at a workshop sponsored by The Center on Learning, Assessment, and School Structure, Philadelphia, Pennsylvania.

Wiggins, G., & McTighe, J. (1998). *Understanding by design.* Alexandria, VA: Association for Supervision and Curriculum Development.

Index

academic outcomes, 31
achievement, 110, 111
activity, as synonym for process, 8
administration, management role in change process, 41
administrative leaders, dialogue with teachers, 81
administrative support, 122
administrators. *See also* Charlottesville (Va.) City Schools
  accountability of, 94
  hiring of, 89
  reconciling conflicts, 57
  role in systemic change, 41–42
advanced learning opportunities, 117–118
affective expression, 22
analytically based instruction, vs. learning profile approach, 29
assessment, 85
  addressing learning profile in, 28–29
  alternative forms of, 11, 13
  bond with instruction, 5
  catalyst for instructional planning, 84
  differentiation in the classroom, 95–99
attention, essentials for, 25
attitudes, 110
auditory modes, 10
Ayers, William, 137

beliefs about teaching and learning, 17
benchmarks, 4
  for change, 36–37

benchmarks (*continued*)
  for different levels of student readiness, 91–92
best practice, 53, 54f–55f, 59, 93
block scheduling, 36
brain research, 12
  identifying point of learning, 19
  learning in accord with readiness, 18
Bruner, Jerome, 18

capacity
  essentials for development of, 25
  maximizing, 17
Carini, Pat, 31–32
centralized direction, as compass for change, 38
change
  characteristics of, 39–40, 47–48
  classroom practice as focus of, 35–38
  districtwide efforts required, 38–39
  efforts linked with wider world, 46
  environment necessary for, 44–45
  imperative in today's classrooms, 34–35
  invitations to, 42
  key players in, 41
  necessity of change in school culture, 43–44
  no end date to, 40
  resistance to, 39
  skepticism about, 39
  systemic, 38–39, 40–42
  tension from, 39–40
change process

Note: References to figures are followed by the letter *f*.

change process *(continued)*
    continuation phase, 94
    implementation phase, 94
    initiation phase, 94
change theory, 33–34
Charlottesville (Va.) City Schools
    developing differentiation plan, 119–120
    district characteristics, 116–118
    factors related to move towards differen-
        tiation, 118
    gearing up for differentiation, 120–121
    implementing differentiation, 124–126
    nonnegotiables in implementing differ-
        entiation, 122–124
    year-end review of implementing differ-
        entiation, 126–129
choice, freedom of, 25
class size, 78
classroom change, encouraging, 49
classroom environment, 85, 97
classroom management strategies, 50, 84
classroom practices, focus of school change,
    35–38
classrooms
    assessing quality in, 100f
    characteristics of excellence in, 53
    diversity in, 1
    need for modern approach in, 34–35
    power of heterogeneity in, 17
    principles related to quality student work
        in, 54f–55f
    respectful environment in, 55f
classroom visits, 83, 84
cluster grouping, 75–76, 123
coaching, 83
collaboration/consultation model, 119
collaborative learning opportunities, 22
collaborative teams, 61
collaborative work, 55f
communication, 22, 104–105, 139, 147–149
community involvement, 46
compacting curriculum, 11, 50, 125
competition against self, 17
competitive grading, 109
competitive learning opportunities, 22
complex instruction, 11
concentration, 20
concept-based curriculum, 91
concept-based teaching, 93–94

concept map, planning for differentiated
    classroom, 2, 3f
conceptual learning, 91
conference attendance, support of, 70–71
constructivist approach, 18
consultation, 83, 84
content
    differentiation of, 7–8
    reflection on, 144f
    selection, 142f
    varying instructional strategies for, 84
continuation stage of differentiation, 50, 87
core groups, 72–73
coteaching, 81
creativity, 20, 25
criteria for high-quality work, 55f
criterion-based reporting, 111
cultural groups, learning style diversity
    among, 28
culture, 12, 26–27, 34, 87
    influences, 20, 21–23
    planning instruction responsive to, 84
    of schools, 43–44
    Western vs. non-Western, 22
curiosity, 20
curriculum
    differentiated relative to discipline and
        grade level, 92–93
    focus on quality, 81
    high-quality, 37f, 54f–55f, 95
    incorporation of model units, 93–94
    levels of, 58
    linking to standards, 92
curriculum design, 91–94
curriculum planning, 126, 127
curriculum tubs, 73
curriculum writing, guidance for, 94

decision making, joint function of students
    and teachers, 7
Delpit, Lisa, 27
Dewey, John, 18
differentiated activities, 142f–143f
differentiated approaches, assessing effec-
    tiveness of, 75
differentiated assignments, identifying, 106,
    128
*The Differentiated Classroom: Responding to
    the Needs of All Learners* (Tomlinson), 11

differentiated classroom, 2. *See also* personalized classroom, responsive classroom
  access to content in, 8
  concept map to plan for, 3*f*
  flexibility in, 7
  goal of, 4
  grading in, 107–113
  leaders' feelings, 12–13
  as means to end, 37–38
  results-based, 47
  social workers used in, 68
  teachers' goal in, 7
  teachers' actions in, 5
  viewing, 69
differentiated curriculum, 75, 90–94
differentiated instruction. *See* differentiated classroom, differentiation
  for basic-level staff development, 83–84
  basis of, 7
  concept map for, 3*f*
  guides for planning, 142*f*–143*f*
  leader's task in implementing, 49
  overview of, 147*f*
  possible indicators of, 54*f*–55*f*
  reconciling conflict with mandates, 57
  research support for, 23–29
  root system of, 16
  underlying beliefs, 17
Differentiated Minigrant Program, 70, 70*f*
differentiated products, assignments for, 143*f*
differentiated programming, overview of, 147*f*
differentiated units, 93–94
differentiation
  addressing classroom excellence, 53
  allocating financial resources for, 62
  articulating vision for, 51–52
  assessing in the classroom, 95–99
  assessing future progress, 62
  barriers to, 43–44
  building understanding and support among stakeholders, 52–53
  characteristics of effective staff development on, 79–82
  clarifying ongoing importance of, 63
  commitment to, 137–138
  communicating about, 85
  conferences supporting, 71
  considerations for potential leaders,

differentiation *(continued)*
  12–13
  content, 7–8. *See also* content
  continuation stage, 50, 87
  coordination with standards-based teaching, 58
  curriculum elements suitable for, 7–9
  definition, 4, 52
  developing shared understanding of, 61
  essential starting point of, 53
  establishing need for, 51–52
  evaluating initiatives for, 56
  evaluating success of, 85
  expanding outside classroom, 2
  as feature of high-quality professionalism, 97
  flow conditions related to, 20
  four-stage framework for change, 50
  framework for, 52
  fundamental role of leaders, 86
  goal of, 62
  grading on growth vs. standard measure of achievement, 107
  growth in, 97
  guidance counselors' assistance in, 66–67
  as hallmark of teacher excellence, 53
  helpfulness of models, 63–64
  high-quality instruction as baseline for, 84
  hiring for, 66, 88–90
  the "how" of, 134*f*, 135–136
  impediments to success, 12
  implementation stage, 50
  importance of developing staff when moving toward, 78–79
  importance to leaders of having supporters, 52–53
  importance of supporting high-quality curriculum and instruction, 81, 82
  initiation stage, 50–63
  instructional strategies to facilitate, 11
  integration into district curriculum, 90–94
  keys to continuing systemic growth, 88
  leadership fostering continual growth, 13
  and learning goals, 54*f*
  likely early supporters for, 52
  linking with best practice, 53, 54*f*–55*f*, 59

differentiation *(continued)*
  in math curriculum, 150*f*–151*f*
  media specialists' assistance in, 66
  misperception of, 52
  modeling, 45
  need for administrative support, 59–60
  outcomes stage, 50
  partnership between specialists and gen-
    eralists needed, 60–61
  personnel-focused strategies, 66–68
  planning for, 62–63
  principles governing, 5–7
  process, 8. *See also* process
  products, 8–9. *See also* products
  providing curriculum to support, 88
  providing teachers with support and
    accountability, 88
  purpose of, 1–2
  qualities of effective communication
    about, 104–106
  quality in, 13
  question-and-answer sheet for parents,
    148*f*–149*f*
  reflections about, 12–13
  requirement for significant progress, 42
  as response to beliefs, 16–18
  in response to interest, 10, 11
  in response to learning profile, 10–11
  in response to readiness, 9–10, 11
  retirees coaching for, 68
  rooted in educational theories, 18–23
  roots of, 16, 17
  service delivery model, 119
  setting stage for systemic growth in,
    50–63
  sharing ideas about, 72–74
  strategies for, 49–50
  structural strategies to aid, 74–76
  student characteristics, 9–11
  support for, 68–71
  synthesis of variety of educational theo-
    ries and practices, 17
  teacher/peer reflection on, 144*f*–146*f*
  technology as central tool in, 67–68
  technology specialists' assistance in,
    67–68
  as umbrella for district initiatives, 57*f*
  vision of, 51–52
  vocabulary and principles of, 2–11

differentiation *(continued)*
  as way of thinking about teaching and
    learning, 13
  the "what" of, 132–135, 138
  as whole model, 30
  in written curriculum, 93
difficulty
  varying degrees of, 9
  working at appropriate levels of, 54*f*
direct instruction, varying, 10
directions, variety of delivery, 54*f*
discussion formats, variety in, 55*f*
discussion groups, 83
district initiatives, focusing of, 56
district leaders, role in systemic change,
    41–42. *See also* Charlottesville (Va.) City
    Schools
diversity
  goal of addressing, 63
  proliferation of, 35
"doing school," 43
*Doing What Matters Most: Investing in Quality
  Teaching* (Darling-Hammond), 78
double-session classes, 59
Dressel, Paul, 109–110
drill-and-practice instructional strategy, limi-
    tation of, 11

Educational Testing Service, 97
emotional independence, 20
English/Language Arts, gauging differentia-
    tion in, 96*f*
*Enhancing Professional Practice: A Framework
  for Teaching* (Danielson), 95
evaluation, local development of, 99, 100*f*
evaluation process, involving all stakehold-
    ers, 102
exempting, 7
exhibitions, as student products, 8–9
expectation-referenced grades, 111
expression, freedom of, 8
extension, 143*f*

faculty groups, prior to implementation of
    differentiation, 120
feedback, local development of mechanisms
    for, 99, 100*f*
feedback tool, expert-generated, 95–97
"fish bowl" discussion format, 55*f*

flexible grouping, 50, 84, 123
  benefits of, 6
  methods of, 5–6
  options for, 6f
flexible pacing, 123
flexible spaces, 10
flow, 20, 26
flyers, in support of differentiation, 74
focus groups, in review of differentiation,
  127–128

Gardner, Howard, 21, 29
gender influences, 12, 20, 21–23, 26, 34
  danger of generalizations about, 22
  female learning preferences, 22
  learning-style diversity, 28
  male learning preferences, 22
gifted education specialists, 130
gifted programs, 117. See also Charlottesville
  (Va.) City Schools
grade-level benchmarks, 111, 112,
  114f–115f
grade-level expectations, 4
grading, 107–113
  competition surrounding, 109
  contemporary approaches to, 110
  equivocal nature of, 109–110
  inaccuracy of communication, 109
  motivation and, 109
graduated rubrics, 125
group investigation, 11
groups, students assigned to, 142f
growth, 17, 110
growth-based evaluation, 110–113,
  114f–115f
guidance counselors, 67, 81, 90
guided curriculum, 81
guided observations, 81
guided work, for teachers, 84
guided workshops, 85

habits, 110
hands-on workshops, 83
heterogeneous classrooms, 17
high-end activities, 127
high-end learners, focus on, 130
high-quality curriculum and instruction, 37f,
  54f–55f, 95
hiring process, 88–90

history, expressing understanding about, 8
Hunt, David, 23

implementation stage of differentiation, 50
independent study, 13, 18–19, 50
individual achievement, 22
individual differentiation diagnostic (KWL),
  141f
individual growth, charting, 4
initiation stage of differentiation, 50–63
instruction. See also teachers
  addressing learning profile in, 28
  in advance of mastery level, 19
  bond with assessment, 5
  characteristics for high quality in, 37f
  differentiating, 100f
  differentiation as element of quality in,
    53–56
  focus on quality, 81, 100f
  moving from specialist-centered to
    shared differentiation, 126
  principles of high quality in, 54f–55f
instructional approach, 119
instructional strategies, 143f
  to facilitate differentiation, 11
  for inviting differentiation, 83
  lack of variety in, 78–79
  varying to differentiate content, process,
    and product, 84
instructional/management strategies, reflection on, 146f
intellectual character, evaluating, 111
intelligence
  fluid nature of, 21
  qualities of, 17, 34
intelligence preference, 20, 21, 26, 28. See
  also multiple intelligences
intelligence profiles, 10
intelligences, 12. See also intelligence preference, multiple intelligences
interest, 84
  differentiating in response to, 10, 11, 84
  as doorway for learning, 19
  enhancing motivation, achievement,
    and productivity, 25
  flow related to, 20
  key to talent development, 25–26
  linked to motivation, 19–20, 25–26
  response to, 37

interest-based learning, 20
interest-based summer activities, 75
interest centers, 50
interest differentiation
    background for, 19–20
    sample research, 25–26
interest groups, 11

jargon, avoiding, 104
journals, 73
joy of learning, 25, 109

Kent State University, 119
kinesthetic modes, 10
KWL diagnostic strategy, 141f

Landrum, Mary, 119, 120
leaders. See also Charlottesville (Va.) City
    Schools
    characteristics of successful change
        agents, 40–41, 43, 44–45, 47
    focusing district initiatives on differen-
        tiation, 56
    helping parents understand differentia-
        tion, 46
    importance of skeptics and antagonists
        to, 52–53
    importance of supporters to, 52–53
    looking for indicators of growth and
        progress, 47
    mission to disseminate excellent prac-
        tices, 38
    needed day-to-day, 59
    need for stability among, 42
    suggestions for maximizing shared efforts
        of general classroom teachers and spe-
        cialists, 60–61
    task in implementing differentiated
        instruction, 49
leadership
    importance on fostering differentiated
        classrooms, 135–136
    mission of, 13
    planning for, 59–62
    support of differentiated classrooms, 12,
        90
leader/teacher relationship, 45
learner need, attending to, 12
learner readiness, adjusting tasks to, 25

learners, differences among, 17
learner variance, attending to, 12, 67–68
learning
    framework for, 58
    joy of, 25, 109
learning centers, 11, 76
learning contracts, 11
learning experiences, choice of, 10
learning goal, focus on, 8
learning profile, 84
    addressing, 28–29, 82
    defined, 26–27
    diagnosing, 84
    differentiating by, 10–11, 20–23, 26–29,
        84
    response to, 37
    among teachers, 80
learning styles, 10, 12, 20, 26, 34
    achievement increased through flexible
        and compatible teaching, 27
    biological bases for, 21
    categories, 21
    matching instruction to, 28
    related to learning success, 21
longitudinal work samples, 107
long-term planning days, 122–123
looping, 50, 75

"mailbox" staff development, 74
mandates, 38, 42, 43, 45, 57–59
manipulatives, 8, 9, 69
materials
    used to develop staff understanding of
        differentiation, 74
    variety available, 54f
math curriculum, differentiation in,
    150f–151f
math manipulatives, 8
meaning, construction of, 12, 18
media specialists, 66–67, 81, 90
memory-based approach, learning profile
    approach superior to, 29
memory-based assessments, positive influ-
    ence of learning profile approach, 29
mentors
    in areas of shared interest, 10
    pairing first-year teachers with, 89
microcultures, 22
minigrants, 69–70

minority groups, factors undermining academic success of, 27
mixed-ability classroom, 75
models, 9, 63–64
model units, 93–94
moderate challenge, 19
motivation, 12, 34
    essentials for, 25
    linked to interest, 19–20
multi-age classrooms, 24, 75
multi-age options, 50
multigrade classrooms, success of, 24
multiple intelligences, 21
    approaches, 29, 50
    Gardner's theory, 21
    Sternberg's theory, 21
multitask classrooms, 75
multitext adoption, 13, 69

newsletters, in support of differentiation, 74. *See also* communication
nongraded settings, 24
norm-based reporting, 111

observational checklist, 124
Ohanian, Susan, 58
opportunity in change process, 43, 45
outcomes
    encouraging change through examination of, 88
    examining, 101–102
outcomes stage of differentiation, 50
"ownership," perceptions of, 61

Paideia seminars, 55f
parents
    communicating about differentiation, 75, 103–106
    communicating about individual learners, 106–107
    conferences with, 106–107
    distributing published grading policies to, 111
    leaders' responsibility to education, 103
    meeting with prior to implementation of differentiation, 120–121
    question-and-answer sheet for, 148f–149f
    skepticism of, 122

parent-teacher communication strategies, 75
part-to-whole approach, 7, 54f
part-to-whole thinking, 22
peer coaching, 9, 81
peer grouping, 10
performance-based assessments, 29
persistence, 20
personal growth, 4
personalized classroom, 2. *See also* differentiated classroom, responsive classroom
Piaget, Jean, 18
planning, 98f
portfolios, 107
    as student products, 8–9
    used in hiring process, 89
preparation, 98f
presentation, variety of modes of, 54f–55f, 83
preservice teacher preparation, 89
principals. *See also* Charlottesville (Va.) City Schools
    hiring of, 89
    role in systemic change, 41–42
    written feedback from, 95
process
    differentiating, 8
    examining, 99–101
    reflection on, 144f–145f
    varying instructional strategies for, 84
product
    differentiating, 8–9
    reflection on, 145f
    varying instructional strategies for, 84
productivity, goal of classroom, 35
professional responsibilities, 97
progress, 17, 110
projects, as student products, 8–9
psychology, learning in accord with readiness, 18
public, communicating with, 103–106
pullout programs, 117, 128

quality instruction, 37f, 53, 54f–55f, 56, 100f
Quest program, 128
question complexity, 55f

readiness, 84, 107–109, 125
readiness differentiation, 9–10, 84
    background for, 18–19

readiness differentiation *(continued)*
    sample research, 23–25
readiness groups, 5
readiness levels, 35, 80
readiness/skills match, 26
reading-buddy arrangements, 7
reading development, continuum of, 114*f*
reading levels, 7, 8
readings, 83
reflective journals, 73
relaxed alertness, 19
report cards, 50, 107–113
reporting mechanisms, 112–113
resources, 9
resource specialists, hiring of, 90
"respectful tasks," 84
responsive classroom. *See also* differentiated
  classroom, personalized classroom
    conditions requiring need for, 30
    mandate for change and, 35
responsive instruction, hiring on support of,
  89
responsive teaching, 38–39
results-based leadership, 47
results-based orientation, 47
reteaching, 7, 143*f*
retirees, 68
rubrics, 9, 11, 97, 98*f*

scaffolding, 9, 18–19, 54*f*, 85
Schlechty, Philip, 35–36
school, as learning enterprises for teachers
  and students, 79
school change
    continuation phase, 103
    differentiation as focus of, 37–38
    implementation phase, 103
    initiation phase, 103
    principles of, 33–34
school culture, 43–44
school-level leaders, 60
schoolwork, 17, 36
self-reliant learners, 85
self-worth, 24–25
service delivery model, 119
shared execution (between teacher and specialist), 124–125
shared planning, 123, 124–125
sharing ideas, importance of, 72–73

single-text approach, 69
site visits, 121–122
skill level, 24
small-group instruction, 54*f*–55*f*
small groups, 143*f*
small-group work, 84
social orientation, 22
social workers, 68, 81, 90
specialists
    crucial role of, 129
    meeting with prior to implementing dif-
      ferentiation, 121
    need for in differentiated classrooms,
      61–62
    role in cluster-grouped classrooms, 76
    roles valued, 127
specialist-teacher cooperation, 72–73
spending, effective targets for, 78
staff development, 50, 121
    at advanced proficiency levels, 85
    alignment with district differentiation
      goals, 82
    based on common differentiation
      vocabulary, 79–80
    basic level, 83–84
    content delivery, 83
    designed for transfer of knowledge,
      understanding, and skill, 81
    differentiating content for, 82–86
    extended study for, 86
    focus on high-quality curriculum, 81
    geared toward grade-level and subject-
      area needs, 80
    importance in moving toward differen-
      tiation, 78–79
    including administrators and district
      leaders, 81
    "mailbox," 74
    mid-level proficiency, 84–85
    options, 125
    power of, 78
    recognizing teacher efforts, 82
    shared, 69
    spanning all phases of change effort, 77
    strategies, 72–74
    teachers' preferred learning modes, 80
    teachers' readiness levels, 80
staff performance appraisals, 129
standardized test scores, 31

standards-based teaching, 58
Standards of Learning (Va.), focus on, 125
Sternberg, Robert, 21, 28
stress, 59
structured observations, 126
student achievement
    related to multiple intelligences
        approaches, 28–29
    related to success rate, 23–24
    related to teacher's diagnostic skills, 23
student assessment, 84
student-centered instruction, 29
student-choice options, 84
student development, 23
student growth, importance of grading on,
    110
student growth plans, 107, 108f
student interest, 82–84
student learning, 45–46
student-led parent conferences, 107
student profile portfolios, 75
student readiness. *See also* readiness *listings*
    addressing, 82
    diagnosing, 84
    pre-assessment, 142f
    response to, 37
students
    access to content, 7
    attention paid to strengths of each, 5
    as collaborators in learning with teach-
        ers, 7
    differentiated characteristics, 9–11
    frustration and disenfranchisement
        among, 2
    growth and success of as goals of differ-
        entiation, 4
    importance of assessing needs, 5
    marginalization of, 35
    working arrangements among, 5
student talent, 10
student variance, 95, 97, 98f
study groups, 72–73, 81
subscores, 111
success, correlated with personal growth, 4
success indicators, 31
success rate, 23
supplementary materials, 69–70
support, planning for, 59–62
support personnel, hiring of, 89

systemic change, 136
    defined, 49
    steps in early stages of planning for, 51
systemic growth, 87
systemic strategies, 49–50

tailoring instruction, 52
talents
    importance of interest in developing, 26
    reasons for development vs. disengage-
        ment from pursuit of, 24
tape recorders, 8
task complexity, 18–19
task orientation, 22
tasks, students assigned to, 142f
task structure, matched to student develop-
    ment, 23
teacher accountability, 94–99
teacher adjustments, effect on achievement
    and attitudes about learning, 25
teacher assessment, 97
teacher assessment tool, 95–97
teacher-centered instructional strategy, limi-
    tation of, 11
teacher-choice options, 84
teacher coaching, 9
teacher education programs, 89
teacher instruction, 97
teacher interviews, 88–89
teacher learning, 45–46
teacher performance, assessment of, 98f
teacher planning, 97
teacher preparation, 97
teachers
    and achievement of meaningful personal
        standards, 58
    as collaborators in learning with stu-
        dents, 7
    characteristics of differentiating, 4
    frustration of, 31, 35
    goal-setting, 97
    hindrances to change, 36
    in implementation phase, 124–126
    influence of preconceptions, 43
    and long-term commitment to differen-
        tiation, 129–131
    methods for ensuring appropriate task
        challenge, 25
    and "nonnegotiables" of differentiation,

teachers *(continued)*
    122–124
    recognition for, 71
    self-reflection, 97
    sources of topics and conditions for staff
        development, 83
    and specialists, 129
    as stakeholders, 120
    student achievement related to diagnos-
        tic skills of, 23
    unprepared for diversity, 1, 78–79
    and year-end reviews, 126–127
teacher-specialist cooperation, 72–73, 129
teacher/student parallels, 79–80
teacher support, 94–99
teacher variance, 95
teaching
    flexibility in, 29
    linking quality and differentiation,
        54f–55f
technology specialists, 67–68, 81, 90
textbooks, 8
Think-Pair-Share, 55f
tiered activities, 11
tiered assignments, 106
tiered lessons, 13, 50
tiered products, 11
time, flexibility about, 22

To Teach: The Journey of a Teacher (Ayers),
    137
turnover, 88, 105

"umbrella goal of differentiation," 56
"uncovering" the curriculum, 58

variances, problems accompanying failure to
    address, 58
videos, 8, 69, 83
vision of differentiation, 51–52
vision statement, helpfulness of, 62
visual modes, 10
volunteer participation, 122
Vygotsky, Lev, 18–19

whole-class discussion, 55f
whole-group instruction, 54f
whole-group work, 84
whole-to-part approach, 7, 54f
whole-to-part thinking, 22
work quality, 110
working arrangements
    for students, 5–6
    variety in, 9
writing development, continuum of, 115f

zone of proximal development, 19, 23

About the Authors

▼

Carol Ann Tomlinson is Associate Professor of Educational Leadership, Foundations, and Policy at Curry School of Education, University of Virginia. She also serves as codirector of the university's Summer Institute on Academic Diversity. Before joining the faculty at UVA, she was a public school educator for 21 years, teaching in high school, preschool, and middle school, and administering district programs for both struggling and advanced learners. She was Virginia's Teacher of the Year in 1974.

Tomlinson is author of several publications for ASCD, including *How to Differentiate Instruction in Mixed-Ability Classrooms*, *Differentiating Instruction for Mixed-Ability Classrooms* [Professional inquiry kit], *Differentiating Instruction, Facilitator's Guide* [Video staff development set], and *The Differentiated Classroom: Responding to the Needs of All Learners*. She has authored over 100 other publications that focus largely on meeting the needs of academically diverse student populations.

In addition to teaching at the University of Virginia, she works with teachers and administrators throughout the United States and internationally on effective instructional and administrative planning for academic diversity. She is currently president-elect of the National Association for Gifted Children.

Carol Ann Tomlinson, Associate Professor of Educational Leadership, Foundations, and Policy at Curry School of Education, University of Virginia. Room 287 Ruffner Hall, University of Virginia, 405 Emmet Street, Charlottesville, VA 22903. Phone: (804) 924-7471. E-mail: cat3y@curry.edschool.virginia.edu

Susan Demirsky Allan is Assistant Superintendent for Curriculum and Instruction for the Grosse Pointe (Mich.) Public School System. She works with teachers and administrators developing and implementing curriculum, improving classroom instructional practice, and inducting new teachers into the teaching profession. Allan is an author of *Local Realities, Local Adaptations: Problems, Process, and Person in a School's Governance,* as well as many articles on grouping practices and gifted education. She has presented at many conferences, served on the boards of national and state organizations, and consulted around the country and internationally.

Allan has served as an educator for 28 years, including positions as a high school social studies teacher, a K–12 resource teacher and gifted education coordinator, a middle school administrator, and a fine arts director. She has also served as an adjunct instructor at the University of Virginia and George Mason University.

Susan Demirsky Allan, Assistant Superintendent for Curriculum and Instruction, Grosse Pointe Public School System, 389 St. Clair, Grosse Pointe, MI 48230. Phone: (313) 343-2069. E-mail: AllanS@gp.k12.mi.us